D1562540

CAPTAIN LIGHTFOOT

The Last of the New England Highwaymen

CAPTAIN LIGHTFOOT ROBBING MAJOR BRAY OF MEDFORD

CAPTAIN LIGHTFOOT

The Last of the New England Highwaymen

MICHAEL MARTIN
and
FREDERICK W. WALDO

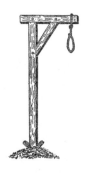

DOVER PUBLICATIONS, INC.
Mineola, New York

Bibliographical Note

This Dover edition, first published in 2016, is an unabridged republication of the work originally published by The Wayside Press, Topsfield, Massachusetts, in 1926.

International Standard Book Number

ISBN-13: 978-0-486-80612-9
ISBN-10: 0-486-80612-X

Manufactured in the United States by RR Donnelley
80612X01   2016
www.doverpublications.com

PREFACE

THE robbery of the traveller in the highway is a trade as ancient as man and oddly
enough has assumed a romantic guise that
has gained the sympathy of contemporaries and
the interest of modern readers. The exploits of
Dick Turpin, Claude Du Vall and others of their
craft have had an astonishing popularity and are
still read with avid interest. As for the highwayman of the Middle Ages, he has now become a
figure of chivalry and Robin Hood and his Merry
Men are considered entertaining characters for
nursery instruction.

In New England, the settlers had no sooner
adopted a "Body of Laws" than they enacted that
any person caught robbing in the highways should
for the first offence be branded on the forehead
with the letter "B." The penalty for the second
offence was branding again and a severe whip-
ping; the third offence was death for the offender.
If the crime was committed on the Lord's Day,
ears were cut off as additional penalty.

Captain Lightfoot, whose real name was
Michael Martin, is believed to have been the last
person in Massachusetts to be hanged for highway
robbery. Shortly before his execution he dictated

to Frederick W. Waldo of Boston, a reporter on the *Columbian Centinal*, an account of his life and adventures which was immediately published and found so receptive a market that three editions were printed within the month following his execution. These were read and reread and most of them were finally worn out so that it has become exceedingly difficult to find a copy with which to appease the curiosity of the modern reader. The present edition follows the text of a copy of the third edition preserved in the Library of the Massachusetts Historical Society.

Sincere thanks are due to Mr. Julius H. Tuttle, Librarian of the Massachusetts Historical Society; Mr. Albert C. Bates, Librarian of the Connecticut Historical Society; Capt. Ernest H. Pentecost, R.N.R.; and to Mr. John H. Edmonds, Massachusetts State Archivist, for courtesies extended in connection with the publication of this volume.

G. F. D.

Advertisement to the First Edition

I WAS induced to undertake the compilation of these pages, by the particular request of MARTIN, and with the sanction of his spiritual advisers. The incidents were communicated by him in a most unreserved manner, and with all appearance of veracity. I have followed strictly the course of the narration, and have avoided as far as possible any attempt at embellishment in the language. It must be apparent, that it would have been impracticable to have set his story down exactly as it was delivered; for many parts of it were so detached and incoherent, that it required much labor to bring them together.

There may be some errors in orthography, as it respects names of persons and places. I have had no time to search Gazetteers and Maps for proper corrections, nor for the admeasurement of distances — I have taken these from him, and used his own pronunciation. Wherever I have had occasion to inquire, I have found him strictly correct. The story, however extravagant some parts of it may appear, is given to the world as the last words of a dying man; and as I verily believe, of one who was determined to tell the truth, and the whole truth.

The object which he had in view, in desiring that his biography might be published, and which he always avowed to me with, apparently, the most sincere earnestness, was, that it might be an example and warning to others. He was sensible that his life had been justly forfeited. That if the promulgation of these memoirs would save, even one young man, from the commission of such crimes, or from meeting such an awful fate, he should consider it some slight atonement, for his numerous offences against the laws of God and man.

It was not until Friday, the 7th inst, the day previous to Martin's attempted escape, that I had completed the business of gathering from his own lips, the materials of his history. From that time I began to put it into a shape for the press. This will account for the delay in its publication, and will excuse the hasty and rough manner in which it is now presented.

F. W. WALDO.

Advertisement to the Third Edition

ON THE 25th of December last, the first edition of this pamphlet was issued; and the demand was so great, that a second was printed a few days afterwards. The increasing interest in favor of it, has induced the publishers now to present a corrected and cheaper edition.

Some omissions have been supplied, and many errors, which it was impossible to have presented, considering the haste in which the first publication was made, have in this edition been corrected.

It was to have been expected, that much doubt and incredulity would have been manifested by certain portions of the community who do not choose to believe any thing that has not fallen under their immediate observation. It would be futile, if not impossible, to argue with such people, or attempt to defend every particular anecdote which has been related. Let it suffice to remark, that there is not one exploit detailed, more remarkable or daring than the two which can be clearly established, and about which there can be no scepticism, to wit: the robbery of Major Bray, and Martin's escape from the prison at Cambridge.

Many violent objections have been made to the

publication of these memoirs, on account of the immoral effects upon society. We shall make no learned disquisitions to shew that the holy fears of such pious objectors are groundless, but would rather express our thanks for their officiousness, inasmuch as it assists the sale of the book. The world is not yet so moral as to shut its ears against the daily perpetration of frauds and crimes. Men, women, and children, must see and hear them. Besides it is a matter of some moment to inquire, whether the ill effects accruing to society from the publication of such a book, by leading others to follow such examples, are not more than counter-balanced by the warnings and cautions which it holds out to the community.

But after all, notwithstanding the bold and successful crimes which are here narrated, and notwithstanding the perpetration of them was cunning or powerful enough so long to elude justice, yet the moral of the tale is, that, *Michael Martin suffered a just and disgraceful death for his crimes.*

January 20th, 1822.

ILLUSTRATIONS

THE LIFE

OF

MICHAEL MARTIN

ALIAS

CAPTAIN LIGHTFOOT

I HAVE in the course of my short life, assumed many fictitious names. My true name is JOHN MARTIN.

I was born in Ireland, in the parish of Connehy, about 7 miles from the city of Kilkenny, on the 9th of April, 1795. My father, Joseph Martin, was a respectable and industrious farmer; and my mother's maiden name was Maria O'Hanlan. They had five children; four sons and one daughter — I was the youngest of the family. My parents were Roman Catholics, and were always considered as virtuous and pious people. They had taken peculiar pains to instruct their children in the doctrines of christianity; and all, but myself, have profited by their religious precepts and example. I was early sent to school, and there instructed in all the first rudiments of education: but, as early as I can remember, I was more fond of diversion and play, than of learning. My temper was violent, and I chose rather to be subject to the government of my own passions, than to parental authority.

At the age of fourteen, I was taken from school, and indented as an apprentice to my uncle, John Martin, who carried on the brewing and distilling business very extensively, at Kilkenny. I might have remained with him, and been treated with kindness, but my bad habits and vicious propensities, disgusted him with me. I was ill-tempered and untractable; frequently beating his children, and quarrelsome with every one about me. At length, my uncle punished me for some crime, and, as I thought, too severely; in consequence of which, I ran away from him, and returned to my father's house, after having been absent seven months. At this time, my evil habits were partially fixed; and I began to indulge in those propensities which have eventuated in my ruin. My uncle followed me to my father, and endeavored to carry me back, and my father beat me severely, to compel me to return with him: but all their threats and entreaties would not prevail — I was determined to stay at home. My father at length consented I should remain, upon condition that I should go to school, and behave correctly; all which I solemnly promised. But I violated all my promises; often neglected my school, and fell into bad company.

At the age of sixteen, being then a forward boy for my age, I joined the "*United Irishmen*," or as they were more generally termed, the *Ribbon-Men*. It is well known that the object of this association was to redress the grievances of our country, and to oppose the government of England. The Irish of the higher classes, who were members of this fraternity in the early periods of the rebellion, were actuated by high and patriotic motives; but in the smaller circles, and in the country villages, they were too apt to make use of the secrets of this association for improper purposes. When I was introduced, by a solemn pledge and oath, into this body, the most profound secrecy was necessary. My father was a quiet man, and did not meddle himself with the politics of the day. I knew he would have discarded me at once, if he had suspected that I had become an United Irishman. When he heard that I had an intention of joining them, he said I was under age, and that boys should not concern themselves with such matters. He often predicted that I should be hanged if I had any thing to do with those folks, who were, generally, the most disorderly and idle fellows in our neighborhood. Their meetings were always held at night, and in some secret, retired place. To prevent my associating with them, he used to lock me into my chamber, before he went to bed.

To effect my purpose, I had prepared a rope

with knots in it, which I concealed under the bed. When I wished to go out at night, I would tie it to the bedstead, and let myself out of the window, after the family were asleep. The meetings were generally appointed at different places each night—sometimes near my father's; and frequently many miles off. I would, when necessary, take one of my father's horses from his barn, and return before daylight to my chamber, by the rope. The association to which I belonged, had secret signs and secret places of meeting, which were changed every night. The time was principally employed in discussing our grievances, in drilling to the use of the pike, rifle and musket; and when those of higher rank had gone, the others would carouse till next morning. Some of those who remained, would talk over the feats of villainy which they had done, or intended to commit. The perpetration of small crimes was directly contrary to the intention of the founders of the association, and in their presence nothing like robbery was ever mentioned. But many others who were desperate in their fortunes, were continually devising schemes to benefit themselves individually, and not for the common good. From such members it was, that I derived my first disposition to mischief and propensity for taking from others what I had no right to demand.

After I had been about six months initiated into this powerful society, my father, who had always been so averse to my joining it, found out that I had leagued with them. His information was received from one of the neighbours, who had frequently followed me to the place of meeting. My father, upon examination, found the rope under my bed, which I had used for escaping, as also some side arms. This provoked him so much, that he seized, and attempted to tie me, for the purpose of chastising me. I resisted, and was very insolent to him. My continual association with men much older than myself, and meeting together under such circumstances, had given me an idea of independence, and I assumed to be a man before I had any right to throw off the yoke of paternal authority. I incensed my father, and he beat me very severely, and as I thought, very cruelly—he cut my head with a stick, and bruised me very much.

I had from my early days been regardless of his chastisement or his admonitions. I had committed many little offences, for which I had been punished. My father at this time, told me that I was an outcast from society, that he could do nothing with me, and that he never wished to see me again. I then formed the resolution, at this time of high excitement, when I thought my father had punished me too severely, to leave his house forever, and told him that I never would come back again.

Very early in life, I had been in the habit of

stealing. I would pilfer from my father, my brothers, and my sister, whenever I could get an opportunity. The severe punishments I received for these offences, never made any impression upon me, but on the contrary, and because they were so severe, I believe that it prompted me to behave worse. However, I do not think that I ever took what did not belong to me, when I was a boy, but that it was soon suspected or known. Sometimes my brothers and sister would keep it secret, upon my promising to do so no more—But I was generally detected by my father, although I had imagined that I had been very cunning.

Some time before this rupture with my father, I had been very intimate with a smith in our neighborhood, named Welsh. He first introduced me to the United Irishmen. He was an unprincipled man, but an ingenious mechanic. In the course of my meetings with him, he endeavored to incite me to dishonest practices. I was pleased with his cunning, and easily fell into his snares. He made for me a key, of a very peculiar form, called a *master-key*, with which I could open almost any lock of a trunk, closet, or drawer. This master-key has been in my possession from that time, till I was confined in the jail at Lechmere Point.

My first essay with this key, was upon my father's trunk, where I knew he kept all his money. I had frequently taken small sums from this trunk, when I found it open; but as I was now determined to leave home, I intended to take enough to pay my expenses. There were upwards of one hundred guineas in the trunk, but I took only five, for fear of detection, if a larger sum was taken away; and that my brothers, who never had any great affection for me, would follow me to Dublin. With the money thus taken, I used to go to some tavern or drinking house, and with my friend Welsh, spend it in dissipation. I gambled when I could get a chance, but in a small way. The only game which I knew, was the *Honest Quaker*; and I was early taught, by my companions, how to cheat at that game.

When I was about seventeen, in the spring of 1812, I started for Dublin: I had one suit of clothes, and carried no bundle with me. Through my intimacy with the stage driver, I travelled with but little expense. I arrived in Dublin, which was about 54 miles from home, the next day. I had never been there before; but I knew the name of the street (Thomas Street,) where an uncle of mine lived. He was my mother's brother; his name was Joseph O'Hanlan. He was a respectable cloth dealer, and lived well.—When I presented myself to him, he asked me whether I had run away from home. I answered, yes; and the reason was, that my father had beat me so cruelly: That I had come to Dublin to seek my fortune, and was willing to undertake any business to get a livelihood. My uncle had known my previous character, and would have nothing to do with me. He said there was no doubt that I had been properly treated, and ordered me out of his house. I left him in a great passion, and gave him much abusive language.

From thence I wandered about the city, till I found out a cousin of mine, who was the head clerk, or cashier, to Messrs. Nicholas, Rowe and Higginbotham, brewers and distillers. They carried on an extensive business. My cousin's name was Thomas Martin. When I went to him, I received no better a reception than from my uncle. At first he would have nothing to do with me; advised me to go back, and told me that Dublin was no place for such a bad young man as I was. I protested to him my repentance for former vices, and my desire to lead an honest life. I wandered about for some days, in dissipation and vice. My cousin met me, and asked me what I intended to do with myself; and still urged me to return to my father. I told him I was going to England.—He said I was a fool; that if I went there, I should either be sent to Botany Bay, or be made a soldier. I answered that I would risk the first, and as to the other, I would die before I would ever wear an English uniform. At length, he thought it best that I should remain in the distillery; I might easily learn the trade, and in a short time get good wages. I consented, and he immediately procured me proper working clothes.

The next day I went to work. I was first put to the pump. — The process was to pump out the whiskey from the larger vats below, into the smaller ones above. I took off the hose from the pump, by which means the liquor all went into the cellar. After pumping for an hour or more, the liquor had almost inundated the cellar, where the furnaces were kept, and the building was in great danger of being consumed. As soon as it was discovered, the foreman came up, and the first salutation I received, was a blow upon the head, which brought me to the ground. I pretended ignorance, and insisted that I did not know how to fix the machinery. My cousin took my part, and was so convinced that it was accidental, that he offered to pay for the loss, rather than I should be discharged. He paid a considerable sum of money; and after cautioning me, it was agreed that I should be retained. I then went to work quite regularly, and acquired a good knowledge of the business. I remained in this establishment about two years; the first part of which, I was very honest and industrious. I afterwards contracted an intimacy with some dissolute fellows, and was in the habit of spending my wages and all other money that I could pick up, in company with profligate men and women. After the first year, I was accustomed to visit a place in

Dublin, called the *Nine Steps*, which was at that time noted as a resort of bad women, and rogues of all descriptions.

The first part of the time I behaved so well, that my cousin was pleased with me, and reposed great confidence in me. He used to send me to his room to make fires, &c. rather than any of the other workmen. In this room he kept the money of the house, and all their valuable papers. The sums of money which I knew were continually deposited there, was so tempting for me, I determined to have a *suck* at the large iron chest—here my master-key was of great service. At first I took only small sums, never exceeding two guineas, for fear of detection; but finding that this money was never missed, I thought I might as well have a *brighter dip*. One morning, in the course of my usual avocation of sweeping his office, &c. I took away about 24 guineas, in gold and bank notes. All this money was spent in my favorite haunts of vice, and being so *flush*, I was always the *great gun* of the company. I went on about a month, taking considerable sums, and spending the money in the same way. The next great *pull* I made, was about thirty guineas, in gold, from a large bag, containing a much greater amount. This I took one evening when my cousin had gone out to a party, and locked all his doors. I found no difficulty in opening any of his locks. I was sorry I had taken so much, both because it might be sooner missed, and because I did not wish to involve my cousin, who might be accused of dishonesty himself.—In the morning, when he went to the bag, he missed some money from it, because the string with which he tied it, was not tied in the same manner as he had left it. His suspicions immediately fell on me. He counted the money, and found how much was missing; he then offered me four of the guineas if I would return the balance. I was very indignant at the charge, and protested my innocence with much passion. He threatened to put me in jail, and actually sent for a sheriff to arrest me; but I insisted so much upon my innocence, and *faced him out* so well, that he said no more about the subject, and told me to go to my work. I plainly saw, however, that he had some suspicion of me, for he did not treat me with so much kindness, and ordered me not to come any more to his rooms. For two months after this affair, I was very quiet and steady; spent no more money, and was regular at my work, for I feared that my cousin had his spies about me, and was trying to detect me in the robbery.

About this time I became acquainted with a handsome young girl, who was a servant in the family of the Lord Mayor of Dublin. The back part of a warehouse, belonging to our establishment, was immediately adjoining the Lord Mayor's garden. The gates were shut at 10 o'clock, and the servants could not go in or out after that hour. I used to have interviews with this girl in the garden, by letting myself down by a rope, from a back window of the warehouse; sometimes would stay in the house with her all night; and in fact, she believed that I intended to marry her. This courtship went on for several months; she always believing that I was sincere, and I going about after other girls when I was not with her. At length she found out that I had engaged myself to three or four other girls, and particularly to the daughter of an inn keeper, where we used to visit. She was very angry, and abused me; I would not visit her for some time. At the end of five weeks, she wrote an earnest letter, desiring to see me, and regretting that any misunderstanding had taken place. She invited me to come the next night at 12 o'clock; and as a signal, there would be a rope out of her window, which would ring a bell, to inform her when I came. I went accordingly: it was bright moonlight, and the night very warm; I pulled the rope once or twice, but heard no bell; at last I pulled violently, and to my astonishment, drew out of the window a quantity of bed clothes. Immediately some person, who I took to be the Lord Mayor, came to the window, and cried out, *"robbery!"* *"murder!"* &c. I ran with all speed towards the warehouse; the servants were soon alarmed, and pursued me across the garden. I had just ascended the rope, and was getting into the window, when one of the pursuers fired a gun, the ball from which, must have struck within an inch or two of me, for I saw it the next day in the window frame. I then pulled up the rope, and went to bed as speedily as possible. It appeared afterwards, that this girl had procured the cord to be tied to the bed clothes of the Lord Mayor, after he was asleep, and to revenge herself upon me, had taken this expedient to get me into a scrape; which if I had been detected, would probably have cost me my life. The next day the sheriff and his officers came to the distillery, and examined all the workmen. I put on as long a face as I could, and escaped all suspicion. I had gone to bed early, with another workman, and got up when he was asleep; so that he testified in my favor, and I in his. They went off without obtaining any satisfaction.

The same afternoon, I met the girl in Fishamble Street. I had determined not to exhibit any appearance of anger at the recent occurrence. I crossed over the street, and was very glad to see her. She asked why I did not come last night, agreeably to her request; I answered that I did go, but went to the wrong place; was affectionate as formerly, and pretended not to care about the misfortune. She promised to keep every thing secret, and I agreed to see her some future time. A few nights afterward, there was to be a dance at the inn where the pretty girl lived, of whom she was jealous—we were both invited there. On the day of the dance, she met with me, and was anxious to know what girl I intended to take with me: I said I should not go unless she would go with me: she replied that she could not leave the house that night, unless she escaped secretly, after the family were in bed. I then proposed to come for her in the usual way, through the garden, and at the appointed hour, I would have a ladder ready, by which we might go over the wall. She assented; and at 11 o'clock at night, she appeared in the garden, dressed out in grand style for the ball. I made the signal to her, and she inquired for the ladder: I observed that I could not procure one any where, and that I had been watched very closely. At length I proposed that she should go out through the warehouse—that I would first go up and let down a rope, which she might fasten round her waist, and I would hoist her up, by means of a windlass, which was generally used for hoisting up goods, in the opposite side of the warehouse. After much persuasion, she consented. She tied the rope under her arms, I hoisted her up about half way to the window, made the rope fast, and went off to the ball, leaving her in that position. She was afraid to make an alarm; and in the morning was found suspended and almost famished. She fainted away when she was taken down; and inquiry was made by the Lord Mayor's people, to find out the person who perpetrated it. The next morning I found the business was rather serious, and thought it would be best for me to *clear out.* I had at that time, not more than a dollar in my pocket; but I undertook to walk back to Kilkenny, leaving all my baggage behind me. My father was glad to see me, after an absence of about two years. He inquired the reason of my coming away; and I always told him it was to make a short visit, and that I should return again. I remained some weeks, very steady and honest, so that my friends thought there was a reformation in my conduct. There was an uncle of mine, named Patrick Martin, who lived in our neighborhood; he was an old bachelor, very rich, and quite infirm. I used to visit him, in hopes that he would give me some of his property. About two months after my return, he died, leaving me but two shillings, and the whole of his estate to my brothers and sister. I was so angry at this, that I would not go to his funeral, neither would I return home; but resorted to my old haunts of dissipation, and to my ancient companions. I staid at these houses as long as I could get credit or money.

My father found me out, and came to persuade me to return with him—I refused. He asked me what I intended to do with myself, and how I should get a living. I said *by my means.* I was very insolent to him—I was not afraid of his beating me; for I had grown so large and so strong, that he would not attempt it. Some days afterwards, my elder brother found me out; and after using much persuasion, and promising to pay all the tavern bills, &c. I consented once more to go home. I then was received with much kindness, and made many promises to amend my life. I went to work on the farm, and was very industrious about three weeks: At which time, I received a letter from one of my old acquaintances, informing me of a grand meeting about 7 miles off; and by the advice of my friend the smith, I was prevailed on to go. I was out all night, drinking, carousing, and listening to tales of the villainy and mischief which had been lately committed. I became ambitious to be as dexterous and accomplished as any of my companions, and was determined that I would not be outdone by any of them. For some days, I *kept it up in high style,* until I had made myself hateful to all the family, and they had become persuaded, that I was too abandoned ever to become an honest man.

My father lived about 4 miles from a market town, and he was in the habit of sending the produce of his farm there. At this time I was in want of cash, and had tried all expedients to raise it. The family watched me so close, that I could get nothing from them. My father had become so suspicious of me and my associates, that he never trusted any money at home; but as fast as he got it, would deposit it in the hands of a rich farmer in the neighborhood, for safe keeping. This man had an iron chest; and the poorer class of people were in the habit of depositing their little earnings with him for safe keeping. We made many attempts to get at this chest, but he was always too sharp for us. My father had five fatted calves in a pen, ready for the market. As the only means I could devise to get money, I, one night, drove these calves from the pen into a bog; two of them I secreted for some days, and the others were found in the bog. After the search was over, I sold these two to a butcher, who gave me about a guinea each for them. I thought this was not quite enough for a *great row;* so I would even content myself to take a short frolic with a girl of my acquaintance. I hired a horse and chair, and took her out to ride a few miles. We were out all night; and in the course of the excursion, I got rather drunk. On our return, I was driving very fast, the horse stumbled and broke his leg. We walked some miles, leaving the horse in the road. I told the owner the circumstances. He was obliged to kill the horse; and as I had no money, I offered to give him my note for the payment, provided he would not disclose it to my father. I gave him a note for 20 pounds; which was worth about as much as the same quantity of brown paper.—He soon after mentioned it to my father, who refused to pay the note, and told him he was served right for dealing with such a vagabond. I then vowed vengeance against that man, and told him he might whistle for his money.

Immediately after this, I was resolved to leave my father, if any means of getting a decent living were presented. The whole family had become disgusted with me, and "treated me like a dog." I roamed about the country for some time, on foot, and visited a relation of the family, who lived about 20 miles off. I was there treated very well, and remained a few days very comfortably. But I began to feel uneasy, and was still desirous of acquiring money, at some rate or other. I turned towards home, being anxious to join my old associates. On my way, I stopped at a public house, which was about five miles distant from my father's. At this time, I was about twenty years of age.

The important part of my history is now commencing. I was at this time little better than an outcast from my own family, and from the honest part of the community. I was vindictive, ill-tempered, and passionate: Yet, at the same time, I was not thoroughly initiated into the higher branches of crime. I was generous in my disposition, and although I had waded tolerably far in iniquity, I do believe, that if I had been kindly treated by my friends, and put out of the way of vicious associates, I should have avoided the snares which have since encompassed me.

When I went to the inn, I have before alluded to, I was much fatigued, having walked a great distance, in a warm summer day. I frankly told the landlord that I had no money, but that I wanted some refreshment. He knew my father, and said that I should have as much as I desired to eat and drink. I sat some time in the bar-room; and in the evening, found that all the company had retired, excepting two men, who appeared, before, to wish themselves alone, and avoided all conversation with the other people. They called for more liquor; and seeing me alone, invited me to partake. I joined them, and we remained drinking and smoking all night. I had never seen either of them before; but one of them very soon discovered that he had known or heard of me.

We retired into another room as soon as I had joined them, and were alone during the night. I said that I had no money. They replied, that was no matter; I was their guest. One of these men, and the least talkative of the two, was a dark visaged, ill looking fellow. I have never seen him since that night, but have often heard of his deeds, though I never knew his name. The other, was an elegant, fine proportioned man, between thirty and forty years of age, about six feet and an inch in height, with an uncommon appearance of muscle and strength. He had fine black eyes, with a wonderful expression; and his face rather strongly marked than handsome. He was dressed like a clergyman; and during the evening, talked as if he was a Priest of the Church of England.

The name of this man, was JOHN DOHERTY.

In the course of this conversation, I thought there was something rather mysterious in his manner, although he appeared to me quite undisguised. But he asked me many questions about my family, myself, and my manner of life, which I thought it impossible for a stranger to be acquainted with. I was not so much surprized that a clergyman should set up all night, and drink and carouse with any of the people, for this was no uncommon thing with the protestant clergy. They were in the habit of spending their evenings in this manner, in my part of the country; and "the bigger part on 'em would drink like fishes." I knew also, that it was common for these clergymen to seek out all places where the Ribbon-men were accustomed to meet; and they were generally considered as the spies of government.

DOHERTY was very earnest in all his inquiries, and was continually plying me with liquor. He asked me at first if my name was not Martin—If I was the young man just returned from Dublin, and who had been obliged to run away from there. "You are a wild fellow," said he, "are you not?" I answered, "yes." "You are very fond of spending money?" "Yes, when I can get it." "You don't much care how you come by it?" "No, if it does'nt cost me much trouble." He said it was a shame that such a smart young fellow as I was, should be at any time destitute of money. He at length wormed himself into my confidence, and

I told him all the history of my past life. After *pumping* me for some time, and finding out what sort of a disposition I had; and after we had got pretty warm with liquor, he threw off his disguise of a clergyman, but did not then tell me who he was. He talked about robberies and religion, alternately; and I was confused throughout the evening, not being able to find out the real character of the man. I questioned him as to his being an United Irishman, and gave him all the secret signs of that fraternity. In the first place, I asked him in Irish, how many buttons he had on his coat? This was the first great watch-word, and the most sacred sign, of the Ribbon-men. He did not either understand the language, or the meaning of the question, when I put it to him in English. I then gave him the other sign, which was simply putting the two fore-fingers of the left hand to the hat. This likewise he was ignorant of; and I was then certain that he was not one of us.

Early in the morning it was proposed that we should separate. The third person went off on foot, after having conversed privately, and taken an affectionate farewell of Doherty. The latter called for his horse, paid the bill, and prepared to ride off. He was mounted on a most splendid blood horse; and his whole deportment and manner commanded respect from those about the inn. He took me one side, and inquired which way I should travel. I told him, directly towards my father's house. He said he was going the same way, and should be glad of my company. If I was fatigued in walking, I should take his horse. So we started off. I walked along side of him, and he continually asking me questions about my family, and the people in that part of the country. When we had travelled a few miles, he proposed stopping at an inn, for refreshment. I rather declined, because I had no money; and also, because I was afraid he might be an Orangeman in disguise; for I could not understand why he was so much interested in my affairs. He insisted that we should go into the inn, and *smash* a bottle of brandy, before we separated. I said I wanted some sleep, for we had been up all night, and were but just recovering from the effects of the debauch. "Pooh!" said he, "I can go eight days without sleep; and if you want a few lessons, I can learn you in a very short time." At length we went in, and he ordered a private room, with a large quantity of brandy, porter and pipes.

In the course of the day, he said he had understood that I was a great runner, and that I could beat many horses. I acknowledged that I had some skill in that way. He proposed that I should try against him. This I considered easy enough because he was so much more fleshy than myself. We had a number of races—I exerting myself with all my might, and he trying to draw me out, to see how much I could perform. He also put me on his horse, to try my skill in riding, and leaping ditches and fences. We spent a great part of the day in these experiments; and he expressed

JOHN DOHERTY, *alias* CAPTAIN THUNDERBOLT

himself much satisfied with my capacity. We went into the house, and after dinner, he ordered in as much liquor as would last us during the evening; desired that we should be alone, and fastened all the windows and doors.

He began by asking me, if I ever expected my father would leave me any money. I said "yes, I expect a child's share." He replied, "you know better—you know that your father dislikes your conduct; that he knows you to be a bad man, and that he will never give you a shilling." He seemed to understand all my feelings, and my situation. He then found me completely in his power, and revealed to me his real character and profession. He said he was a highwayman, and that he was CAPTAIN THUNDERBOLT. I was astonished and alarmed at this information—I had for many years heard of the daring exploits of that man; and his name had for a long time been a terror to that part of the country. He had been often advertised; and but a few days before, I had seen an advertisement offering a reward of £500 for his head. I then felt a little dread at being left alone with a man of whom I had heard so many outrageous crimes, and was anxious to get out of the room. He took out two large pistols, and laid them on the table, after cocking one of them, and said, " Martin you *must* stay with me, I cannot part from so clever a fellow as you are." I then sat down again, and he urged me to drink more. He then recounted many of his feats; some of which were so amusing, and apparently so innocent, that I listened with great delight to him. *He touched my quality exactly*. But above all, I was interested to find how he had accumulated so much money, and with so little trouble. He made a great display of his watches and jewels and money. He offered me his purse, saying that I was a *lean pigeon*, and that would help to *oil my wings*. I objected to receiving the whole of it, and took only six guineas.

I remained till near midnight, hearing him recount his adventures, and he persuading me to embark with him. At about 12 o'clock, there was a great tumult in the yard of the inn—he opened the shutters to see what was the matter: He said it was a party of dragoons, probably in pursuit of him; told me to keep quiet, and meet him at a certain place which he designated, about three quarters of a mile off. He had scarcely made the arrangements, when I heard among the confusion of voices in the lower room, (for we were in the second story,) the name of Capt. Thunderbolt repeated by many of them. By this time, he had made his escape out of the window.

In a few minutes, a noise was made at the door of the room, and a peremptory demand for admission. I perceived the object of their pursuit, and thought I might gain some time for my new friend, if I parleyed with them. After keeping them for some minutes on the outside, and strenuously denying that Capt. Thunderbolt was in the room, they burst open the door, seized me, and carried me down stairs, intending to detain me as an accomplice. I denied all knowledge of the man; and fortunately, the landlord happened to know me and my family, and through his exertions I was liberated. After remaining some time, and finding that they had missed their object, they went away, and in a different direction from that which I was to take, to meet Doherty. I moved off immediately, and found him at the appointed spot. I advised that he should go with me to my father's barn, which was but a few miles off, where he might sleep in the hay-mow till morning. He agreed to go, after extorting from me a solemn pledge of secrecy. I found no difficulty in getting into the barn and shewing him the way to bed. I gave his horse a large quantity of grain and hay, and told him that it would be best for him to be off early in the morning, before the family were moving. I directed him to the ruins of a Monastery, about a mile off, across the fields, where he would be in no danger of interruption, and where I would meet him in the morning.

This being arranged, I got into the house through a window, and went to bed. About 12 the next day, I started to see him, and had much trouble in procuring provisions from the house, to carry him. I succeeded at last, in *lifting* something from the kitchen, for him, and some grain from the stable, for his horse. The night before, he had cautioned me not to approach him, without giving a certain whistle, which he instructed me in; for he was armed, and might fire upon the first intruder. He had with him a fine pair of double barrelled brass pistols, a dirk, and in his portmanteau, a large blunderbus. When I arrived at the ruins, I saw his horse tied to a tree; and after reconnoitring, I saw him asleep in the ruins, upon some bushes which he had gathered, and his blunderbus along side of him. I gave the signal, and he awoke instantly.

We went out into the fields, and sat down to eat the food which I had brought him. He soon renewed the old subject, and urged me to become a partner in his trade. He said, that under his direction, I should get a good living, which I could do in no other manner. I replied, that I had no fear for myself; but, notwithstanding I had been treated so unkindly by my family, I did not wish to bring them into disgrace. He ridiculed all these notions, said that "his family were nothing to him; they had discarded him long ago; and he was counted as the lost one." I held out for a long time, and positively refused to go with him. He then proposed that we should have some liquor, and requested me to get some. I was rather afraid to go to the next tavern, as I had no smaller money than a guinea: the landlord knew my character, and would either accuse me of having come by so much money dishonestly, as guineas were not very plenty in those parts, or else he would take the balance of it for some money which I owed him. So I went back to my father's, and procured a small boy, who went to the inn and bought a quart of brandy, and returned the change. We drank this in the Abbey. We spent three or four hours in this place; and as I was determined not to join him, I advised him to go away, for I thought they had watched me from my father's house. I took a solemn oath, that I would never divulge what he had said to me; although I had then made up my my mind that I would not become his partner. He said he should return again to see me, in a week or a month, or perhaps never. It depended upon the closeness of the pursuit, when he should meet me again. He gave me the signal, and we appointed the place of meeting. He would inform me by letter, when he should come back, and so we parted. I then went home, and lounged about among my old acquaintances, and my family took no notice of me.

In about a week, I received a letter from Doherty, informing me that he would be at the appointed place in three days; at which time I went, and found him on the spot. At my first approach, I was much surprized, and doubted whether he was the same man—But as soon as he had given the signal, I knew him. His person was much changed — He had put on quaker's clothes, with long grey hair, and his face painted quite pale. He had also another horse, and looked very simple, and apparently, indisposed. I remained all night with him, in an old cabin that was unoccupied. He soon began the old topic of urging me to go with him; recounted many other particulars of his life; and said that I would never be taken while I kept with him, and followed his advice. He said, it was his principle, to make property equal in this world. That he would get as much as he could from the rich, but would never molest the poor—He would take money from those who had more than they knew how to use, but would never take life, if he could avoid it. If there was any danger of detection, or any strong opposition, he thought himself justified in taking life. These were the principles which he laid down to me; and which I have generally followed. He said, although he had been the terror of Ireland and Scotland, and traversed England in pursuit of money, he had never taken away life; had never maimed any one; and, with two or three exceptions only, had never drawn a drop of blood. He had been married five times—all his wives were then living; and from some of them, he had received considerable property. But he had appeared under different characters and names. Sometimes he was a priest, then a pedlar, a quaker, and a soldier, a beggar, and a huntsman. At this interview, I was induced to associate my fortunes with his; and it was agreed that we should commence the campaign on the following morning.

This eventful day was in the month of July, 1816. I was about twenty one years of age—as smart as a steel trap, and as strong as a bear. Capt. Thunderbolt gave me a long morning sermon, upon what I had to do, and how I must act. He initiated me into the order, by first throwing a glass of brandy in my face, and calling me *Captain Lightfoot*. He then presented me a double barrel brass pistol — after having drawn the charge, and loaded it again with slugs, he told me to put it in my bosom, and while I kept with him, and observed his instructions, I should never be taken or die. I obeyed most willingly, for my whole soul was with this man, and I thought he would stand a pretty good tug with old Satan himself. I was not sorry at leaving my father's house, where I was never welcomed with affection—But I never once thought that the treatment I had there received, was the consequence of my own dissipation and vice.

We started early in the morning—Doherty on an elegant bay horse, and I on foot. We took an opposite direction from my father's, and halted about five miles off, at an ordinary ale house, for breakfast. He informed me that there was to be a great hunt a few miles off, and there he expected me to make my first *dip*.—After breakfast he put me on his horse, which he said was named *Beefsteaks*, and he walked by my side for three or four miles, when I gave up the horse to him. There was to be a grand assembling of all the nobility, gentry, and officers, in the neighborhood, at this hunt, and Doherty had found out the place of meeting. As we approached the spot, we met a number of the country people and servants, with horses, on the road. D. said they were not worth stopping, for "we must shoot higher than that." His object was, to get me a good horse, and another dress, from some of the gentry, who he knew never went armed to these meetings. When he thought it was time for *the game* to come along, he gave me my instructions; we shook hands, and swore to stand by each other till death. When any thing worth examining approached us, he was to separate from me, and stand by the road-side; and with his quaker dress, pretend to be frightened, if there should be any slight skirmish; but if it looked serious, he was to step in.

At length we met four men, on elegant horses, having the appearance of great men; some dogs with them, but no servants, and riding very leisurely. "Now," says he to me, "I shall try your pluck—You must go up boldly to the outside one, present your pistol, and demand his money." I rather doubted, thinking it almost too bold to encounter four men. He said, "you must not be afraid if there was an hundred—none of them are armed, and half of them are cowards—I know them all." Immediately he took position in the ditch, by the side of the road. I went up resolutely, and presented my pistol to one of them, who proved to be Lord Powerscourt, and said, "deliver me your money." Three of them halted, but the farther one put spurs to his horse, and was off like lightning. Lord P. seemed rather frightened, and said he had but little money about him. I told him I had heard that he carried it under his saddle, and that he must dismount and let me examine. He hesitated, until I seized the reins, and drew the horse round from the others—still keeping my pistol near his body. He then dismounted, and I as quickly leaped into the saddle. I then ordered the other two to dismount, which they did instantly. I then presented the pistol to another, and demanded his purse, which he quickly gave up. All of them were somewhat intimidated, and were watching the quaker, who was trembling in the ditch, as if they suspected him to be an accomplice. One of them seemed to be a little more impudent than the rest, and I went boldly to him, and told him to *hand over* his watch—He did so. I then said to Lord P. "I should like to exchange coats and hats with you." He handed his first, and I retreated towards the quaker until I had taken off my own, still keeping the pistol pointed towards them. I handed them to him, but did not wait to put on his garments then. He asked me if I was *Captain Thunderbolt*—I said, "no, I am his brother, *Captain Lightfoot*." I then bid them good morning, and we rode off across the fields, got into the woods, where we divided the spoil, and I rigged myself out in the huntsman's dress. The quaker praised my bravery, and said, "I had taken the first brush like a true game chicken." We then moved off across the country, avoiding all public roads. He knew the whole country, and I trusted to his direction. Our horses were both hunters, and we found no difficulty in leaping fences and ditches. We went with all possible speed towards Dungarvan, a seaport town in the county of Cork, which was upwards of 40 miles from the place of our departure. We halted in a wood, about a mile from the town, early in the evening. We had found a place where we could be secure for the night; and Doherty sent me into the town to procure some refreshments. He said it was necessary that the horse which I had taken, should be christened in due form, and therefore I must get some liquor for this purpose. I went into the town, dressed as a huntsman—rode up to one of the principal inns, and without dismounting, called for a quart of brandy and some cold meat and bread. All this was readily furnished, and I paid them well for it—put spurs to my horse, and pushed off to join the Captain. We went through the regular ceremony of christening my horse — He was named *Down-the-banks*, by the Captain, he pouring some brandy into his ears.

The next morning we went towards Cashel, which was about thirty miles distant. We travelled very moderately, and stopped at a number of public houses; but we fell in with no game on the road. This part of the country was too far out of the way of the *shining gentlemen*, for we met with none but petty farmers and *old hens*, who carried no change about with them. Instead of taking from these people, the Captain frequently

MICHAEL MARTIN, *alias* CAPTAIN LIGHTFOOT

dismounted at a cabin where he saw the appearance of poverty and distress, and gave something to the inhabitants.

Before we reached Cashel, Doherty changed his clothes, for he always carried three or four different suits about with him. He put on an ordinary dress, and acted as my servant, for I had on a gentleman's splendid hunting dress; and unless I spoke much, as he told me, I might pass for as good a gentleman as any of them—"For," said he, "Lightfoot, only put on fine clothes, have a plenty of money in your pocket, swagger a good deal, but say nothing, and you may pass through the world as a great man." We went into the town of Cashel, I following his directions. He told me to look big, and he would keep watch whether any one was in pursuit. We went to a private house, ordered the horses to be taken care of, and went to bed early. We were off the next morning at sunrise. After we had rode about 20 miles, we overtook a funeral of some poor peasant, and the people about the corpse looked so poor, that Doherty threw them some money, and I did the same. He proposed to dismount and assist them; but he had scarcely spoken, when looking back, he discovered a party of horsemen, their uniform shining through the bushes. "Now, brother," said he, "we must run the gauntlet, for the red coats are after us." It was a party of about twenty dragoons, that had tracked us all the way, notwithstanding our change of clothes. He immediately leaped a ditch, and set forward over fields and bushes. I followed him. The soldiers almost cut us off, and fired at us several times. They were so near that one shot struck Thunderbolt's saddle. However, as they had but common dragoon horses, and ours were good hunters, we soon distanced them.

We travelled very rapidly towards the city of Galway, and did not stop till night. We then halted at a small village called Clonloghan. We went to a tavern; I ordered supper, and said my servant would attend me, and eat after I had done. We fastened the door, and sat drinking till late at night, expecting that we should be pursued. Early in the morning, I ordered the horses and paid the bill. I was informed that my horse was lame, and that he could not stand. I told the people to take good care of him, and I would send my servant after him in a few weeks, and would pay all expenses. I said I should use my servant's horse; that he would walk part of the time, and I the rest, till we reached home. The landlord said he could procure me a horse in the neighborhood. I doubted whether any one would hire me a horse, as I was a stranger, and had never been in that place before. He asked me where I was from. I answered, from Galway—That we had been out hunting for some days, and that I had missed the rest of the company. He said there would be no difficulty in procuring me a horse, which I might keep till mine was well. He then went off, and brought a handsome looking horse, which I mounted, and we rode off in an opposite direction from Galway. This horse was not equal to Thunderbolt's; and we were obliged to go slower than we could have wished, on that account. We went that day, to a village called Kilmallock, about 30

miles distant. We stopped at a tavern, and called
for a chamber to ourselves. I wished to have another change of clothes; so I went into a tailor's
shop, the only one in the place, and ordered a suit
to be made immediately. He called all the boys
and girls in the neighborhood, and went to work.
In about two days he had completed them, and I
paid him well for the clothes. During this time,
we kept quite snug in the house, for we had heard
of the advertisement about us, and some of the
pursuers actually passed through the village, while
we were there.

At day break the next morning, we decamped.
Thunderbolt thought it was best to avoid the part
of the country where we had been before; and
therefore, proposed that we should go towards
Cork. There was a probability of picking up some
game in that quarter. About 2 o'clock that day, we
drew up to an inn, where he discovered a number
of soldiers and constables. He immediately gave
me the signal, and we wheeled off. They commanded us to stop; and set out after us. Some of
them mounted their horses, which were standing
at the door, and followed on. They fired at us
three or four times; but we got out of their reach
in a few minutes. We travelled that day without
refreshments, and as fast as our horses would carry
us. That night we remained in an obscure cabin,
and the next day reached Cork. I was never at
Cork before; and was ignorant of the people and

city. Capt T. had been often there, and thought we should be more secure in the outskirts, than in the city itself. So we rode through the town, and took up our quarters at a small inn, about two miles out of the city, and put up our horses at a large livery stable in the city. We staid at this place three days, drinking and carousing, without venturing to show ourselves in the city. My horse died the first night, from being rode too hard. When we were about going off, Capt. T. sent a boy to the stable, with a half guinea, to pay for the keeping of his horse—He was afraid to go for him himself. The boy returned, saying, that the man would not give up the horse to any one but the person who came with him. He then suspected that it was a trick to entrap him; and proposed that we should clear out as fast as possible, which we did on foot; taking the direction to Donerale, which was more than 30 miles distant. We arrived there that evening, and put up at a small inn—We went into a room by ourselves, and ordered something to eat and drink. We spent that night there; one of us watching, while the other slept. We had seen in the bar-room, an advertisement, offering a large reward for our apprehension, and describing us minutely. No one could be mistaken in Capt. T.; and the landlord looked suspicious on our first entrance — So we kept ourselves private. The next forenoon, while he was asleep, I was sitting at the window, in the back part of the house, and saw a number of people, perhaps about twenty, approach the house; among whom, I could discern some soldiers, with side arms in their hands. I immediately pulled Capt. T. by the whiskers, told him my suspicions, and we started down stairs. As we were going out of the door, the landlord attempted to stop the Captain, and said, "you must pay me the scot." "I'll give you my note for it," said the Captain, and immediately knocked him down. We went off, over the fields, as fast as our legs would carry us. The soldiers pursued, and fired upon us—One ball struck the Captain in the calf of the leg, and impeded his running for some time. However, we managed to get out of the reach of the pursuers, and travelled over the country about 10 miles; when he was so exhausted, that it was impossible for him to go any further. We concealed ourselves in a wood;—he fell down on the ground, and as I thought, was a dying man. He had sense enough after a few minutes rest, to tell me that there was a small bottle in his pocket, which he directed me to give him. He smelt of it, swallowed a few drops from it, and rubbed his head with it. He was soon revived, and directed me to take out the ball from his leg, with my penknife. "Cut as near the lead," said he, "as you can; I can afford to lose a little blood." It was the first time that I had ever officiated as a surgeon; but I saw he was so resolute upon the subject, that I cut it out without any fear. He bound up the wound himself, and said we must remain in that wood some time. I cut down a quantity of bushes to make a bed for the Captain, and we remained in this situation for about twenty four hours, without meat or drink. The medicine that he carried with him, saved his life; for he had bled profusely. The next night, I left him, to go in pursuit of food. After some hours search, I went as a beggar to a gentleman's house; they were all gone to bed; and when I awoke the servants, they refused to give me any thing, at that time of night. I waited a little while, and then made a *plunge* at his fowl house, and brought away a brace of turkies. With some difficulty, I found my way back to my companion. I made a fire by means of our fire arms, and roasted one of the turkies—I ate very ravenously; but he abstained, although he said, he was quite hungry. "If he was at the most splendid banquet in the world," he said, "he would neither eat nor drink—That abstinence was the shortest way of curing his wound."

The next day, I started again, in pursuit of some provisions for myself—but the moment I was entering a farm-house, I was hailed by a man, who looked like a bum-bailiff. I did not answer, but took to my heels. He pursued, and raised an alarm; but I outran all the people that he had summoned; and taking a roundabout direction, arrived at the place where the Captain lay; after an absence of five or six hours. Early the next morning, we moved from the wood. He thought he should be able to walk, with my assistance; and if we only got one mile further, it would be safer for us. We travelled slowly all that day. He was acquainted with the country, and knew precisely, what rout to take. He leaned upon my shoulder, and hobbled along all the day. When it was near night, we had got near to a small village. He laid down in the bushes, and directed me to go to an Apothecary's shop, for a certain medicine, which he knew would be serviceable; for he seemed to have studied physic, as well as every thing else but religion; and that, I am sorry to say, he did not know much of — Although when occasion required, he could talk a great deal about it. I went to the shop, procured the plaister and other medicines, according to his directions, and got from a small shop, something to eat and drink. We staid in this place, the rest of the day; and at night, moved again. After two or three hours walk, we came to a plantation, where the grounds were laid out in a handsome style—The Captain knew the place; and we went to a fox cover, where he was satisfied we might rest secure, until his wound would allow him to travel faster. The first time I ventured out in pursuit of provisions, I met a number of men on horseback, who looked rather suspicious—I evaded them, and returned to our retreat, where we remained nearly three days, without any refreshment but water. On the third night, I ventured out again; and after examining very cautiously, I came up to a small farm-house, and asked for some food. They gave me some cold meat and some beer. The woman of the house was preparing supper. I told her I was a poor travel-ler, and had no money to pay her for the food, of which I had already devoured a large quantity. She was making a quantity of *Stir-about*, (or as it is here called, hasty-pudding.) After she had poured it out into a large dish, she went out of the room, for some other purpose. I catched up the dish, and went off with it to my friend, who was, by this time, nearly exhausted. This lasted us, with economy, for two days. After which, I tried the like experiment at another farm-house, where I paid them for a quantity of the same food. We were afraid to kindle any fire in the woods; and besides, the Captain knew it was best for him to abstain from all animal food or ardent spirits. We continued more than a fortnight in this place; during which time, I really felt much sorrow for the course of life I had commenced. I used to cry frequently, and wish myself at home as an honest man. Whenever I had these feelings of repentance, he would ridicule me, and say, "your hand is in now, and you may as well play the game out—if you go back, you will be laughed at and disgraced; besides you would not now leave me alone, in this situation." I was often determined to separate from him, and run the risk of detection; but the idea of leaving him in his trouble, and the arguments which he used, determined me at last to stay. In an evil hour, I renewed the former oath, that I would never part from him if I could avoid it.

At the end of a fortnight, he was able to walk very well, and we went off eight or ten miles through the bogs, where we took up our abode in a *Shanty*, for about a week. On the road, we fell in with a number of bog-trotters, who gave us some provisions, and we paid them liberally for them; for, although we had many opportunities, yet I believe that both of us were too good natured to steal a halfpenny's worth from these poor people. We travelled on, soliciting charity from the peasantry, till we came to Clonmell, having rested for one day only, at Lismore.

At Clonmell there was a court in session. There were about 15 criminals on trial; some of them were United Irishmen, that I had heard of before. One of them gave me the sign; and I immediately suggested to the Captain that we might rescue one or more of them. The greater part were sentenced to be transported to Botany Bay, and two of them to be executed. We took up our quarters at the most celebrated inn in Clonmell, where the judge was, and other respectable people. We tried many plans to liberate some of the convicts, but were always defeated. The judge had some strong suspicions about Doherty, and cautioned the landlord to be on his guard against both of us. We found out this by the assistance of a girl in the house, and were determined to be revenged upon him. We remained here as snug as we could, for three or four days, till the assizes were over.

The judge travelled in a coach and four, and his servants were well armed. We ascertained that he was to start early in the morning; and at night we broke into the stable, and took out the linch pins from the after wheels, and so disguised the place, that the coachman could not suspect that there was any thing out of the way. In the morning we moved on about two miles further, and remained in a small grog shop, waiting for the judge's coach. We had been there more than an hour, when we saw the four horses coming by most furiously, with only the forward wheels of the carriage. We immediately started back, and met the servants in pursuit of the horses. We went on to the place where the accident had happened, and found the carriage broken to pieces, and all the neighbors gathered around it. We tried to *lift* something, but there were too many spectators. No accident had happened to any one but the coachman, who had broken his leg; and we contrived to slip a guinea a piece into his hand, and pushed off, sorry for his misfortune, but regretting that we could get nothing from the judge.

We then considered it best to take the sea-coast

towards Dublin, and to reach that city as soon as possible. We travelled without interruption or suspicion, for three days; and paid at the taverns for every thing we called for. Early the next morning, we met with a gentleman and his servant, each on horseback, who we afterwards understood by the advertisement, was Sir William, [the name not remembered.] Captain T. went up to him, and taking off his hat in the most respectful manner, said, "I have a letter for you, your honor." He was then riding slowly, and reined in his horse. As soon as he had stopped, the Captain put his hand in his pocket, came close to him, and drawing out one of his large pistols, said, "I want your money and your watch." He hesitated, and asked some questions; when the Captain seized the reins with his left hand, and said "quick! or you are a dead man." During this dialogue, I had taken the opposite side, and presented my pistol to the servant, which kept him from interfering. Sir William handed over an elegant gold watch, and his purse, containing upwards of thirty pounds in gold and silver and bank notes. The servant, with great trepidation, took out his watch, which was an old silver one, and some small change, and offered them to me—I told him they were not worth taking, and if they were, I should not deprive a poor fellow like him of them. "No," said the captain, "we are not in the habit of troubling any but gentlemen." He told the gentleman that he was in need of some small change to settle a few private accounts; that they need not be afraid of their lives, for although he had presented a pistol, he knew he could get what he wanted without drawing blood. "However," said he, "we shall only put you to the trouble of walking a few miles—so both of you will be good enough to dismount—We want those fine horses of yours, and we shall return them to you, when we have done with them." They made no attempts at resistance, but quietly dismounted, and we as quietly took their places; and bidding them a pleasant walk, pushed off with all speed.

We travelled very rapidly in the night time, and laid by during day—keeping the sea-board towards Dublin. We fell in with nothing that was worth taking; and heard nothing of pursuers or advertisements. On the fifth day, near ————, about 50 miles from Dublin, having been so long disappointed of game, we came up to a splendid mansion house, belonging, as the Captain said, to a Mr. Wilbrook. "Here," said he "it is possible we may *nip* something; for if we don't have some business soon, our hands will get rusty." After telling me to follow him, and be as bold as he was, he led the way up the avenue at full speed —rode up to the door, and asked if Sir John Barker lived there. This was a fictitious name, and the servant replied, "no, this is Mr. Wilbrook's place"—"Oh, that is the gentleman I wished to see—is he at home?" "No sir, he has just gone out on a hunt." "Are any of his family at home?" —"Nobody but his two sisters and the servants."

He then alighted, and, in great style, ordered the servant to take care of our horses. I followed him into the house. He walked into the hall and ordered the servant to call the ladies: He addressed them in a most polite manner; said that he lived not far off—that he had been robbed the night before, and from the best evidence he could obtain, that a servant of Mr. W. had been concerned in it. He desired that he might just see them; and the ladies immediately ordered the whole family to be assembled in the hall. They came in singly, he examining each of them, and saying, "that is not the one," till he had got them all collected; when he opened the door of a small room, and told them to walk in there. At the same moment, he drew two pistols, gave me the signal, I drew mine, and told them all to sit down in that room—that the first one that stirred should be shot. I guarded the door, and he asked the ladies to walk into the opposite room. He told them his trade; that he wished to do nothing to them but what was gentlemanly, and would not take from them a farthing of property; but he had understood that there was a valuable treasure in that house, and they must *shell out*. He laid his pistols on the table—asked for a glass of brandy: They gave it to him in great fright, and he used every means to prevent them from being alarmed. After some time, they went up stairs, and brought down a gold watch, a pocket book, containing bank notes, and a purse, with a quantity of specie in it. Doherty said that this was not all the treasure; he must have more. They went again, and returned with watches and jewels of their own. He said that he would rather be burnt to death, than take any thing from a woman. He told me to lock the door. We took each of us a part of the spoil, kissed the ladies, and bid them good bye. After we had mounted our horses, I threw down the key of the room where the servants were confined; and we took our course across the country, avoiding the public roads. The amount we lifted at this house was about 160 guineas.

We then rode off towards the hunting ground, and stopped at a tavern, where many of the huntsmen passed by. We saw three men coming down the road, but before we could mount they were out of our reach. We jogged along slowly over the fields, till we crossed two gentlemen, mounted on elegant horses. Doherty rode up, drew a pistol, and said, "Gentlemen, we wish to exchange horses with you; so the sooner you dismount, the better for your carcasses." After they had dismounted, I demanded their watches and money: The Captain said, "No, brother, we have got enough for the present," and rode off. He was so prudent, that he was afraid to wait long enough to *take* any thing, for fear that the other sportsmen would come up.

We were now well mounted, and thought we could get out of the way of any thing. We had money enough, and if we could avoid pursuit, we expected to live well for a few weeks at least. We endeavored to avoid public roads, and made our way across the country towards Waterford. The second night, we put up at a small tavern in a village called Corquaan: ordered supper, and that our horses should be well taken care of. While we were at supper, (as I found out afterwards,) there came an advertisement of the last robbery, describing us exactly. I knew nothing about this; and just as we were preparing to go to bed, I went into the kitchen, to have a little chat with the girls, leaving the Captain alone in the front room. One of the girls told me that the landlord was suspicious of us as being the great robbers, and that he had sent out for the constables and soldiers. D. was almost asleep, and thought that all this time I was upon the look-out. The girl had scarcely given me this information, when I heard a noise in the entry; and going out to see what was the matter, I saw a party of dragoons, headed by the landlord, with an axe in his hand. I saw that my assistance would be of no use to my friend, and thought it best to provide for my own safety: so I leaped through a window, which happened to be closed. This was the only means of escape I had; and I met with no other injury than cutting my face and hands a little with the glass. I got into the garden; was pursued round the barn, and just as I was mounting a high fence, two of the soldiers fired—I fell, although not at all injured, and laid still, on the other side of the fence. They considered they had killed me, and came up with a lantern: I kept perfectly still, and they kicked me about and examined me; at last went away, saying, "we have killed one of them; let him wait there till morning." As soon as they had gone back, "*I cleared out like a rigger.*" I believe that I must have run more than an hour, before I stopt a moment. I took an opposite tack, and got into the main road, where I lay concealed for some time in the bushes. I had almost fallen asleep, when I heard a great noise of footsteps and conversation: I remained quiet, and presently a great crowd approached; some on horseback, and some on foot, with lanterns and fire-arms. In the centre of the gang, I could discover Doherty, apparently tied to the horse, and a number of soldiers on each side of him: He had a white sash round his hat, by which he could be more easily known at night.

After the procession had passed, I got up, and followed on, about three miles, to the magistrate's house. On the way I went into a small cabin which was deserted—the occupant having joined in the tumult. There I disguised myself as well as

I could, by blacking my face and altering my clothes. I then made my way among the crowd, and witnessed the examination at the magistrate's. The Captain's arms were tied behind him, and his feet tied together. After a short examination, the justice was satisfied that he was the notorious Thunderbolt; and as there was no jail in the neighborhood, he ordered him to be confined and guarded in his house, till the next morning. I went off with the rest of the crowd, after having found out what was the strength of the guards.

I concealed myself in the rear of the stable until midnight; and then, by the assistance of my pistol, struck a light, and set fire to the stable. I then cried fire, as stoutly as I could bawl. The whole family were alarmed by the conflagration of the hay, and most of the people who were guarding the Captain, came out to assist in extinguishing the flames. I watched the opportunity, and found out in what room he was confined. I went in, and there were only three soldiers left to guard him. I found them sitting quietly along side of him, their muskets placed in the corner of the room. I drew both my pistols, and swore that I would kill the first man that started. They seemed terrified, and offered no resistance. I took out my knife and cut the cords with which the Captain was bound, and gave him one of my pistols. When he was getting up, one of the soldiers got up and grasped a musket; but before he had time to cock it and present, I fired my pistol and shot him in the leg. I did not intend to kill him; but as I was so near him, I knew that I might wound him in the leg, which would answer my purpose. He fell — the rest were still more alarmed, and we pushed off on foot, leaving them to mend their legs, and put out their fires, in the best manner they could. To be sure we missed our horses; but we had no doubt that we should be mounted again before the next night.

We travelled the greater part of that night, towards Ballyhagen, in the easterly part of the county of Meath. Towards morning, we rested in a nursery or grove, of a gentleman farmer. About nine o'clock, we saw an elegant horse walking slowly down the road, at some distance from us. As we approached, we saw that it was a groom, who was training the horse. The Captain went up to him, and ordered him to stop, which he did. He told the groom that he wanted that horse, and he must give him up directly. The servant refused, saying that it was his master's favorite horse, and he should be punished if he lost him. Without any more ceremony, the Captain took hold of his foot and pushed him over the other side. He then mounted the horse, and told me to get up behind him. In this manner we rode for more than two days, stopping only for slight refreshment, and following the sea-shore, to keep out of the way of public roads. During this time, we fell in with nothing worth taking. We slept in the ruins of an old building on the third night, and avoided all public houses; for whenever we ventured to stop, we saw ourselves advertised. The next night, being within about 30 miles of Dublin, the Captain told me he would put me in the way of mounting a good horse; for we were already fatigued with riding double. He pointed out the residence of a rich sportsman named O'Brien, and said, if I would venture into his stable, I might find a good horse. I tried to enter a wicker gate at the back part of the garden, but found it was fastened: I tried the master-key, but it would not succeed. At length I burst it open, by running against it, and went silently to the stable, which I found also locked. I heard the noise of the horses, and was determined not to leave the spot, unless I brought one away. I succeeded in climbing up to a window, by means of a long pole, which was lying in the yard—broke through the window, and got into the hay-mow. While groping about in the dark, I fell through a rack among the horses, and broke the third finger of my left hand, which I have never since had the use of. It was so dark, that I found myself in danger of being trod upon by the horses; nevertheless, I went round among them, and felt of them all. I at last pitched upon one that seemed the most restless; and by feeling of the hoofs, I found it was a young one, and had never been shod. After feeling round for a bridle or halter, for a little while, I thought I heard a noise of some person, as if snoring in their sleep. I kept still for some time; and after all was quiet, I put my pocket handkerchief round the neck of the horse, and coming to a door which was fastened inside, I moved off with him. I soon rejoined Thunderbolt, who said I ought not to use that horse, he was too wild for me to manage. I insisted upon trying him—took the saddle and bridle from his horse, and mounted him. The horse set off like lightning, and I had no power over him — he took the direction towards the house, and as we approached the wicker gate, I saw lights and people in the yard, making a great bustle. The horse was about entering the gate, when I put my right foot between his shoulder and body, which stopt him at once—He fell, and I brushed off, leaving the saddle and bridle. The people pursued me instantly, and I took an opposite course from the place where I had left the Captain. I was obliged to jump into a pond to avoid pursuit. There was so much mud that I could not swim; however, I waded through it, and in less than an hour joined my friend. When I came up to him, my voice was so much altered by fatigue and fright, that he did not know the signal, and was upon the point of firing at me. I kept still some minutes, when I recovered my voice, and he knew me. He was obliged to leave his horse behind, because I had lost the saddle and bridle, and he left him tied to a tree. We set off on foot. After we had gone rather slowly for an hour or more, we heard the sound of a waterfall. We went to it—he told me to take off my clothes, and we would wash the mud out of them. I stood naked there for some time, till we had washed them, and wrung out all the water that we could. He said I must put them on, that the heat of my body would dry them—This was not very comfortable, but still I endured it through that night. In the morning we went into an ordinary farmhouse, got something to eat, went to bed, and moved off as soon as we awoke, which was about noon. By this time my clothes were dry, and I could travel as fast as the Captain. He was acquainted with all that part of the country, and we staid that night at an old comrade's of his, who lived in a very retired place, not far from the Dublin road. Here we were well received, and thought it best to remain quiet for a day or two. But after the first day, we thought the fellow acted rather strangely. He talked about the large rewards that were offered for us, and the Captain began to smell a rat, although this fellow had been under great obligations to him—So he gave him some money, to go and buy some whiskey, and as soon as he was out of sight, we cleared out, taking the Dublin road.

The next morning, as we were walking very leisurely by the side of the road, we met two gentlemen in a dashing gig—We put in our watch chains, and pulled our hats over our faces. When they came up, Thunderbolt touched his hat, and made a low bow. They stopped. "Will your honor please to give me the time of day," said he. The gentleman who was driving, then pulled out his watch. The Captain immediately presented his pistol, and demanded their watches and money. At the same time, I stood at the horse's head, with my pistol, and threatened to shoot the horse, if they dared to move. They were both Englishmen, and one of them was an officer in the army, I think I heard afterwards, that his name was Colonel Brierton—the other one looked like a nobleman.

The officer asked if we were really in want of money. The Captain replied, "yes, we are very poor, and you Englishmen have made us so. You had better be quick." One of them said, we will give you all we have. The other began to ask questions, and kept looking behind him. He asked if we meant to take every thing from them. Thunderbolt said, "give me your watches first, and then I will be after calling for your purses to pay the taxes upon them." The officer handed his watch slowly, and I observed that he was feeling with his right hand for something behind him. I suspected they might be armed, and instantly advanced towards them, and threw my pistol at the officer, which struck him in the head—He was senseless for some time—The other fell down in the gig, and begged for his life. We both sprang into the gig, and dragged them out—One of them was quiet enough, and Doherty gave the other a blow on the head with his fist, which settled him. We then stripped them of their money and their gold watches—The money amounted to about fifty guineas. They had papers about them, of no value to us, which we would not take—Their money was our great object.

We drove off with great speed; but had not got far, when Doherty stopped the horse suddenly. I asked, what was the matter—He said, he hoped neither of those men were killed. We looked back, and saw one of them moving, and trying to raise up the other. We waited till we saw that both were able to stand, and then drove off as fast as the horse would run. We went about five miles; and although it was early in the day, we were afraid to be overtaken on so public a road— so we fastened the horse to the hedge, and started into the fields. We went to the house of another acquaintance of Doherty, and remained there for two nights, without any suspicion.

When we were about going away the next morning, we offered to pay for our supper, &c.— He would receive nothing, he said, from his friends; but, he said, if we had any spare money, it would be a good deed to assist a poor neighbor of his, whose stock and furniture were about being taken for tithes. We went to this man's house, and saw him and his large family in great distress, expecting every moment to be turned out of doors. The captain asked him how much was demanded by the minister. He said there was upwards of forty pounds due, and he had no means of payment. Suppose, said he, I lend you the money—will you be able to pay it in one year, when I call again? The poor man thought he should be able. The Captain gave him the money, and refused to take a note from him; but told him he must be sure to take a receipt from the minister, or whoever else he paid the money to. We waited some time at this house, until we saw the minister and the excise officer approach the house. We then went off, by another road, about two miles, expecting they would return that way immediately. I went off about dark, to a farm-house, and got some provisions; but not so far off, that I was out of the reach of his signal. We remained in a lime-kiln, near by the road, all night. In the morning, about 8 o'clock, we saw the old fellow approaching, with the excise man, both mounted on good looking horses. As soon as they came up with us, we separated, taking opposite sides of the road. I went up to the minister, and said, "I have a letter for you sir," at the same time offering him a piece of blank paper, folded up. They halted, and the Captain presented a pistol to him, and demanded his money. I then made the same request of the other man. The parson said he had no money about him; that he was a poor man. "You lie," said the Captain; "are you not ashamed of yourself?—I didn't know that you pious protestant gentry would lie so. I know you have money about you, and that you came by it improperly, so please to restore it to its lawful owner." The parson was very obstinate, and prepared to make resistance. He called upon the other to assist him; and he was upon the point of moving, when I put my pistol close to his body, and said I would kill him if he stirred a limb. This kept him quiet; but the parson was more refractory, and somewhat insolent in his language. Doherty finding that he was about getting away, fired his pistol, which was loaded with small shot and salt, and wounded him in the thigh—He did not intend to do any thing more than disable him for a few days. He fell from his horse, and the Captain took from him the same guineas that he had given the poor man, the day before, together with a few pieces of silver, and his gold watch; which he said, was enough for the interest upon the sum he had loaned. The horses were not worth taking; so we made the best of our way towards Dublin, on foot, always avoiding large taverns, and the most public roads. We went to the house of a widow, where we asked for lodging; the Captain pretended to be very sick, and we staid at this house about a week—It was retired, and we kept out of the way of all persons.

While we were at this house, we heard much

conversation about a rich widow, who lived in the neighborhood, by the name of Macbriar. She was represented to be a very weak and ignorant woman, yet lived in great style. She had been a poor country girl, but had married a rich old bachelor, who lately died, leaving her a handsome estate. I had been much too intimate with the daughters of the poor woman, at whose house we were staying, and had promised marriage to one of them; so that nothing was said before them, about our intention towards the rich widow. However, the Captain had planned it, that we should go off immediately to Dublin; that I should get the most elegant clothes, and return in great style, to court the widow. I objected, because I knew nothing about talking to ladies; and perhaps, should not behave myself properly. "Nonsense," said he; "I can tell you words enough in two minutes, that will answer your purpose to make love to any woman in Ireland. You are a good looking fellow, and have got plenty of money; and you will be well received, if you only look bold, and talk large." I consented to make the experiment, and he gave me a few lessons how I should behave. We left the poor woman's, paid her generously, and started for Dublin. We went into the inns on the road, very boldly; but generally heard something about Captain Thunderbolt, and saw advertisements, describing both of us. Soon after we left the house, where we had been secreted so many days, we met a servant on a miserable horse, and stopped him, to ask some questions about the roads, but not with any intention of robbing him. He said he was a servant of a major; and that he was carrying his uniform from the encampment to the next village, to have it repaired. It is the very thing I want, said the Captain, provided it will fit me. He ordered the fellow to hand it out. He hesitated a little—but upon the Captain's shewing the muzzle of a pistol, he threw off the portmanteau. The Captain tried on the coat—it fitted—he handed the servant his own—took the remaining part of the uniform, and gave the servant two guineas in exchange, and told him to push off, in the opposite direction. He was then completely rigged out as an officer; and we passed through the country without much interruption. At the village of ———, about fifteen miles from Dublin, we stopped at an inn, to dinner, and remained there some hours, drinking at a very extravagant rate. They took him to be an officer. Shortly after dinner, he went out to the stable, and in a very grand manner, ordered the ostler to saddle the two best horses in the stable. We paid our bill in the house; and when we returned to the stable, we found the horses ready for us. No questions were asked, and we rode off, without any ceremony. We reached Dublin that night, and put up at a large inn, in the outskirts of the city. The next day, we went to a tailor's shop, and I purchased an elegant suit of clothes, for the purpose of visiting the widow. The Captain got a suit of black; and when he returned, laid by the uniform. In a few days, I had received sufficient instruction: and from the inquiries we had made in her neighborhood, about her connections in Dublin, we had prepared forged letters of recommendation; and I sat out upon the expedition. The Captain was to stay at Dublin, till I returned.

I went back in great style, with a servant that I had hired for a month—Went to the house, and was well received. I remained in the neighborhood more than a fortnight; and we concluded a bargain of marriage. I described myself as being very rich, and owning large estates in the vicinity of Dublin. She was prevailed upon to go with me to visit my family in Dublin. She sat out in her carriage, with three servants; and when we arrived in Dublin, every thing was prepared by the Captain, for our reception. He had hired an elegant house, and got together a number of people, who were to pass for my relations—He was to act the part of my father. She remained there but one day, when she was anxious to visit her friends in the city. I made an effort to prevent this, because the whole scheme would have been blown up, so I prevailed upon her to return to her own house. We went off, having got the consent of my pretended father and mother, to our union. I remained at her house for four days; when one

The Widow Macbriar

evening a pedlar came there, offering his goods for sale. I was walking with the lady, and I knew his face at once. He had seen me at Kilkenny, and knew my character. I made the best of my way back, with an intention of bribing him to secrecy; but before I had come up, he had asked the head servant, why his mistress was walking with that rascal. He told him my real name—that I was a notorious highwayman, and a companion of the famous Thunderbolt. As soon as the lady returned, the whole camp was in confusion. She was very outrageous, and sent off some of the servants for the peace officers. I found that I was getting into hot water, and decamped with all speed.

I arrived in Dublin the next morning, and found that the Captain had been watched very closely; so we moved off to the suburbs of the city, and remained some days in a small tavern; regretting the failure of my love adventure. We remained *housed*, for ten days; when we heard that there was to be a grand wedding, not far from the poor woman's house, where we had remained so long. The Captain said we had been still for a great while, and suggested that we should go to the wedding—That I should dress up in woman's clothes, and he would attend me. He would fix me out, and give me all proper instructions. We started for the woman's house, where we knew the daughters could procure me proper garments. We gave them money, and they purchased the clothes for me. We went to the wedding, and found a great number of people entering the house; we joined in the crowd, and got in without any molestation—nobody thought of asking whether we had an invitation or not. I passed off very well for a woman, had a veil over my face, and said but little. After the supper was over, a collection was made, according to the custom in that part of the country, for the benefit of the priests. The Captain put in as liberally as any of them. We started off when the company began to disperse, and found out that the four priests had come there in a carriage, with only one servant. We went on about half a mile, and waited in ambush, till the priests' carriage came up. We started out into the road, and the Captain seized hold of one of the horses' bridle. I presented a pistol to the driver, and commanded him to get down — he obeyed. The Captain opened the door of the carriage, and presenting his pistol, demanded all the money and jewels that they had. They asked us if we were robbers—He answered that we had the honor of following that trade. They gave us all the money they had with them; and while they were feeling for it, one of the priests talked about the impropriety and sin of such conduct. The Captain told him, that was no time for a sermon; he would come to his chapel and hear him preach some other time. We lifted about sixty guineas in this adventure, and went off to the house where we had prepared for the wedding. I had left my own clothes there, but was careful to take the money and watch with me. As we approached the house, we saw it surrounded by a large number of people, some of whom appeared to be soldiers. We immediately suspected that the girls had betrayed us, probably out of revenge to me, because I had not fulfilled my promise of marrying one of them. We went very cautiously towards the house, but as it was a moonlight night, they discovered us, and made an outcry. We ran off through some bushes, and they pursued us very closely—fired one or two guns, but didn't *graze* us. I ran fastest, and he took to the river. Although I could swim very well, I had rather trust to my feet. I lost sight of Doherty at the river, and pushed on till I found that nobody was following me; then laid down in the woods to rest. About midnight I walked near a mile, when I saw a light in a hovel, and went in—there was a poor family, all asleep in the same room. I said I had lost my way, having been thrown out of a chaise in coming home from a party. They made no objection to my remaining there; and in the morning cooked me a good breakfast, and I pushed off. On the road, I saw some people at work in the fields; their jackets and hats were on the ground, not far from the road. I was anxious to get rid of my female dress, so I watched an opportunity to walk off with some of their clothes. Fortunately, I had kept my pantaloons on, when I played the lady, so that a jacket and hat was all the additional dress I needed. I made a selection of the best I could find, and this was bad enough: however, they were of so much value to the owner, that the men seeing me remove them, set up a shout, and followed me. I had dropped a half guinea where I had taken the coat and hat, which was really good pay enough for the clothes. They did not overtake me. I pulled my clothes up above my knees, and was out of their sight in a short time. They gave up the chase, and I went into the bushes; there changed my clothes, and put my female dress into a bundle. I kept concealed for more than two days, without any thing to eat or drink, but water from a small brook.

At last I came out of the wood, and inquired of some poor peasants the road to Dublin. They gave me the directions, and I went on till I reached a small farm house, where I went in, to procure some refreshment. There was no one in the house but a young woman and a little child. She gave me something to eat, and some whiskey, which I paid her well for. I then shewed her the bundle of clothes; she was very much pleased with them, and said she would buy them if she had money enough. I asked her if there were any men's clothes in the house that would fit me. She said that one of her brothers had a suit, nearly new,

which would just do for me. She brought them—
I made the exchange—kissed her, and went off
towards Dublin, by the circular road. This was in
the summer of 1818.

I changed my clothes, and gave away the old
ones to a poor fellow that I met in a by-road. For
four days I remained quiet in a small tavern, not
more than five miles from Dublin, and the next
morning went towards the city. In a short time I
saw a gig coming towards me, with an old gentleman and a boy in it. This was the first carriage I
had met that morning. I recollected his face, and
knew him to be a doctor that I had frequently
seen in Dublin. I took up a large stone, catched
hold of the reins, and stopped the horse with my
left hand. I told him I should kill him with that
stone, if he did not quickly deliver up all the money that he had. He was alarmed, and the little boy
cried. He threw down his pocket book on the
ground. I took the reins out of his hand, and told
him to sit still, that he should not be harmed; it
was only his money that I was after. I opened the
pocket book, which contained a number of papers;
took out all the money I could find, which was
about nine pounds in bank notes. I then asked for
the watch—he handed out an old *silver* one. I
told him it was not worth taking, and handed it
back to him, with his reins. He asked me my
name. I told him it was David Brimstone, and
that I should burn him up if he didn't whip up

and brush off directly—"If you look back I shall throw this stone at you." He was glad enough to get off, and I bid him good morning.

I got into the city without interruption, and went to a tavern in Little James Street, where I staid during the day. I heard much talk about the Captain; and found out that he had been in the city lately, and had *borrowed* a purse from a nobleman, at the theatre, three nights before. I went about the city that night, to see if I could pick up any thing, but avoided all that part of it where I was known. I saw an auction shop open, and went in out of curiosity. I saw a fine pair of brass pistols hanging up—waited till they were for sale, and bid them off. I then went to a small shop in Thomas Street, bought a sufficient quantity of powder and ball, and went round to different inns, to find out something about Thunderbolt. At one place, I heard them reading an advertisement about him; and one or two observed that he had been traced almost to Kilkenny. I listened very attentively to the conversation; stood in the back ground, drinking my liquor. Presently I saw some of them whispering, and their attention directed towards me. However, I tried not to show any embarrasment —paid for my liquor, and walked out of the bar room very deliberately. As soon as I had got into the entry, I heard expressions, saying, "that's his comrade;" "that's the other," &c. I thought I should be followed, so I run up stairs with all speed, got out on the top of the house, and there loaded both of my pistols, which I had concealed in my bosom. I remained there more than an hour, ready to meet any one that should come. At length, I supposed that if they had pursued, they had not examined the house, and I ventured to descend. I saw a light in the upper rooms, and was somewhat alarmed, till I saw that it was only a small girl, with a light in her hand. She took me to be one of the family, and I took the candlestick from her, saying I wanted to go to bed. She went down stairs without suspicion. I then pulled off my coat, and tied it up in a handkerchief. I saw a box in one of the chambers, containing a quantity of meal or flour. I put some of it on my hat, my clothes, and my head—then went down stairs, with a broom stick in my hand for a cane. When I reached the lower entry, I saw a number of people there. I pretended to walk very lame, and passed out of the door boldly, and without any suspicion on their part. I got into a retired street, and there put on my coat, and walked off towards Kilkenny. Towards morning I rested a few hours at an inn; and when I called for breakfast, was surprised to hear them tell me, that they were not in the habit of entertaining highwaymen. I suspected that they had traced me there, and as soon as I got out of the house, I walked very fast, and had not proceeded many yards, when on looking back, I saw four or five men running after me. I then took to the fields, and went off upon the *full drive*, for about two hours, till I was out of danger. I slept in the woods that night; and in the morning was crossing the grounds of a rich landlord, when I met a servant, who told me that his master did not suffer any person to go over his grounds; he said he was a surly old fellow, and if he met me he would shoot me. I did not much care for this; but had not proceeded more than a mile, when I was interrupted by the man, who ordered me to go back again. I said that I had business that way, and must not be stopped. He lifted up his cane, and was about striking me—I very quietly gave him a *sinker*, and went on, leaving him on the ground.

In two days I arrived at Castle Dermot, which was about twenty miles from Kilkenny. I knew all that part of the country, and many people about there, so that I had no difficulty in keeping myself secreted. In a few days I heard of Thunderbolt, and was told that there had been a hot chase after him; and that he had robbed Sir William Morris, who was my father's landlord. I then went in pursuit of him, towards Kilkenny, but keeping out of the way of my relations in that part of the country. I met a great many people who knew me, and called me by name, but I denied that I had ever been there before. I had painted my face, and put a patch over one eye, and changed the color of my hair, at Castle Dermot—

Yet my voice and walk betrayed me to many who
had known my tricks before. There was, however,
no attempt made to arrest me; for although they
had thought me a wild fellow, they would not believe that I was an accomplice of Captain Thunderbolt. At almost every place I stopped, I met
with some of the association, so that I was sure of
protection. In a day or two, I heard some people
talking about the Captain—I said I was a con-
stable, and offered a large reward to any person
who would tell me where he was. An old man,
who sat quiet in a corner of the room, when I went
out, followed me, and gave me the old sign. He
said he wanted no reward, but believed he could
shew me that night, to the place where the Captain was concealed. At night, during a violent
storm, we went out, and walked about 3 miles, to a
small hut. He went to the door, and after knocking some time, a man came armed with a blunderbus. My conductor said something to him in a low
voice, which I did not hear, and began to be suspicious. At length I gave him the signal of the
Ribbon-men, and asked him in Irish, if Thunderbolt was there—that a friend of his wished to see
him. Doherty came to a window with his pistols
in his hand, and demanded who was there. I knew
the voice, and gave him our watch-word immediately. I went in, and we all staid there that night,
carousing and drinking till morning. We had been
separated about five weeks, and he was very glad

to see me. He had been more successful than I had; for he had borrowed upwards of six hundred pounds, in gold and paper, besides five gold watches.

In the morning we thought it best to clear out. He said he was well known in all that part of the country, and that we had better make our way to the north of Ireland, and *walk off* with the first good horses we could find. If there was no game in the north, he said he should push off directly to Scotland, where we might find something; or, at any rate, be out of danger. Our first object was to get well mounted, for we were both well armed. For two days we travelled without success, and without danger—We avoided the great road to Dublin, and meant to take the most private way to Bangor or Belfast. On the third day, we saw a gentleman on an elegant horse, and perceived no one near him. I walked up to him, with my pistol cocked, and told him to stop instantly. For what purpose, said he. "I want to rob you; so you may as well *shell out*." At that moment, a servant came driving up to us, and blustering pretty largely. The Captain stopped him before he approached, and said, "if you advance another inch, you are a dead man." He halted at once. The master then handed me out his pocket book and purse—I told him, his watch would be no trouble to me, and he handed that, likewise. There was about 70 pounds in the purse and pocket book. The servant was much frightened; and the Captain came up to us, to see how I got on. The gentleman asked him if he was not Captain Thunderbolt—"Yes," said he, "I am the very boy." He asked me in a very polite manner, for his watch—that the money he should think, was enough for our purpose. I told him it was rather too pretty for him, and that my wife was in need of such a one. I went towards the servant, and told him to get out of that saddle directly—I took possession of his horse, and he stood trembling, by the road side, begging for his life. I threw him some small change, and said, that I never injured such fellows as him, and only requested that he should keep still. The Captain very politely asked the gentleman if he would be kind enough to dismount — You are better able said he, to ride in a stage coach than we are. He obeyed, and we rode off.

When we had got out of reach of pursuit, we buried our spare money and watches; each one keeping to himself, where he had deposited his particular property. I have omitted to mention, that we have done this two or three times before. Some of this money we have taken; but a great part of it is concealed to the present day.

Our object now was, to get to the north of Ireland; and if there was nothing to be obtained there, we might cross over to Scotland, where we should be out of the way of danger. We pushed on as hard as our horses would carry us, (and they were very excellent ones,) across the country, avoiding Dublin. After about four days travel, we reached Lisburne, in the country of Antrim; we made no attempt at robbery on the road, for we had no time to spend in small matters. At Lisburne we staid but one day, as the landlord suspected us, and intimated that we were rather of the doubtful order. To be avenged of him, we returned at night, and as our horses were rather worn down, we took the liberty of exchanging them for a fresh pair, in his stable.

The next morning, we borrowed a purse from an old fellow, who was riding alone, in a miserable gig. The Captain asked him the road to Belfast — He told him to "find out by his knowledge." This provoked me; and I immediately went up on the other side, and demanded his money. The Captain called me off, and said I should get myself into a scrape, by lifting any thing from such a poor devil as that. So we moved off; and he whipped up his horse, threatening that he would have a file of soldiers after us directly. I then put spurs to my horse, and followed on about half a mile, before I overtook him—I pulled out a pistol, and told him to give up every thing he had. He protested for some time, and begged for his life. I then dismounted—having taken out a knife, I cut his reins, and fastened my horse to his gig. I was determined to strip the old fellow, on account of his insolence. I jumped into his gig, took him by the throat, and commanded him to *shell out.* He said that he had only a small bag of gold, that he was carrying to Lisburne, for another man. Upon examination, I found a considerable quantity of money, amounting to £150 — with which I made my way to the place where the Captain was waiting for me.

That night, we got to Belfast, and went to a large inn—After we had taken our supper, we went round the town, in pursuit of game—Fell in with nothing of consequence. In the morning, the Captain said we had better go over to Scotland, and try our luck there. We chartered a small vessel, the Captain of which, agreed to land us at any port on the Clyde, that we should wish. We put our horses on board, and embarked immediately. There was a violent storm, and it was two days before we crossed the North Channel. We landed at a small town called Presswick, and paid the man handsomely for our passage. We staid there quietly, for some days; and then the Captain proposed we should try our luck again. We went towards Glasgow, and met nothing on the road. He thought it best not to trouble any body for the present. At Glasgow, we passed ourselves for Irish gentlemen; and offered to sell estates in the county of Waterford. The Captain exhibited a number of deeds, and was very near concluding several bargains. Two persons, at least, he sent over to examine the lands, and gave them letters of introduction to ——, people in the moon. We swaggered a great deal, spent considerable money, and remained in G. about 3 weeks. One morning the Captain saw a gentleman preparing to go out in a gig—he knew him, and said he was going to his country seat, and no doubt had a considerable sum of money about him. We followed him some miles before there was an opportunity to stop him. The Captain rode up, and said he wanted to borrow a few shillings of him. "Begone you rascal," said he—"Stand still you rascal," said the Captain, "or I will blow your head from your body"—drawing a large pistol at the same time. The man was alarmed, and asked how much would satisfy him. All you have got, said I, coming up on the other side. He gave up his purse, which contained only about nine pounds, and we could not stop to examine him particularly.

As we were going away, he asked the Captain if his name was not John Doherty. He said it had been, but that I had given him a new name, which was Captain Thunderbolt. He was an old schoolmate of the Captain's, and advised him to abstain from such a vicious course of life. He said that he had heard of his tricks, but if he would let him retain his watch, he would pledge his honor that he would never expose him. We suffered him to retain his watch, and pushed off.

We then steered towards the Highlands, and were prowling about that part of the country for more than three weeks, and met with nothing of any consequence. We found that advertisements had reached this part of the country; and as we were watched so close, it was considered best to go back again towards Glasgow. We patroled all that part of the country, and did not meet with any person who carried more than a guinea about him. The Captain was acquainted with all that part of the country, and was often called by name in the public houses. He was obliged to assume different disguises; and as I was not known, and could lie tolerably well, we escaped detection — although we had run many narrow chances.

We then came to Queen's Ferry, not far from Edinburgh, and did not attempt to take any thing on the road. The Captain was disguised, because he was well known in these parts. He had a visor on, and long grey hair; so that very few could distinguish him, unless he was on foot, and then he was afraid that his large figure would betray him. One evening at Queen's Ferry, there came in some persons who looked like spies. One of them asked another, if he had heard that Doherty had returned to Scotland — and they watched him very close. I pretended not to know him, and joined in the conversation—asked them if the person they were talking about, was the famous Captain Thunderbolt. I told them he had been hanged in Ireland lately, for murder. I made up so fine a story about it, that they really believed it; and the

Captain went out of the room, while we were conversing—I followed in a few minutes, and found him in the stable, with the horses ready — We mounted and made off as fast as possible. He was afraid to go to Edinburgh, as he had at first proposed; for although he had not been in that part of Scotland for four years, yet he found that he was suspected. We took a circuitous rout to Glasgow. We first went to Linton, then to a small place called Crawford, near which the Captain was born. He went to the house of his sister, who was a widow, where we remained secure for some days. This sister knew very well the Captain's mode of life; but as he always supplied her liberally with money, she never said any thing about it. Our next journey was towards Glasgow. The horses were refreshed, and we went very leisurely, examining almost every thing that we met on the road; but found nothing worth taking. We remained but two days in Glasgow, and picked up but a little change. It was growing too hot for the Captain; and we started off towards the mouth of the River Clyde. We met with a party of dragoons, who asked some questions, to which we made no answer, and they suspected we were either deserters or robbers. As we were moving off they ordered us to stand—but we had finished all our business with them, and bid them good morning. We set off at full speed, and they pursued us very closely for about five miles. We undertook to swim our horses over a small river, where the current run very strong. I got safely to the opposite bank, but Doherty's horse was about sinking, for he was so heavy that the horse could not swim with him. Finding that the current was carrying him fast down the river, he threw himself off the horse, and swam ashore. I followed down by the side of the river, and as soon as he came ashore, he mounted behind me, and we set off again. We travelled all that day and night, stopping only once for slight refreshment. The horse was at length beat out, and we tied him to a tree by the side of the road, knowing that we could go faster on foot. We made towards the River Dee, where he hoped to find some better trade going on. At a small village, we bought a quantity of medicines, and an old suit of clothes each. He was to pass for a travelling physician, and I as his apprentice. In this disguise we travelled about the country, for seven or eight weeks; the Captain had so much skill in medicine and surgery, that we picked up a good deal of money. He had a number of quack medicines, and having *a good gift of the gab*, he could pass them off very well among the natives. He told them frequently, that he "was a capital hand at *bleeding*, and that I was just getting my education in the same art."

This disguise kept us out of the way of suspicion; and as it was an honest and innocent trade, I was sorry that we could not follow it through life. I said one day, to the Captain, that I had rather go on in this way, and would never take to the highway again. He laughed at me, and said, "to be sure we can get a living in this business; but money is not worth much to us if we can't spend it. I want to lay up enough, so that I can get into some other country, and spend it like a gentleman—Besides, I like the fun of frightening the loons, and taking from them what is of no use to them." He became tired of his profession of a physician, and said it was time we had got into better business—So we started again for Glasgow. We arrived there without committing any robbery, and went to a house of ill-fame, where we remained four or five days, drinking and spending a great deal of money. The Captain then proposed that we should return to Ireland—He said there was no game in Scotland, for they were old fowls, and never carried much treasure about them. The evening that he proposed this, we met a gentleman in the streets of Glasgow, who looked as if he might have something to spare. It was bright moonlight, and we saw his watch chain glittering. We followed him, till he had got into a retired street, and then demanded his money, both of us taking him by the throat. He was so frightened, that he could not stand—We very soon lightened him of his watch and purse; and seeing some people approaching, made off. In the morning, there was a great alarm in the city, and advertisements that a man had been knocked down in such a street, by two men, nearly murdered, and robbed of a very large amount. We kept still all that day; and at midnight went to the quays, in pursuit of a vessel that was bound to Ireland. After a long search, we found one. There was a smack lying at one of the quays, with two men on board, asleep. We awoke them—presented a pistol, and told them they must set sail for Bangor. They said the owner of the vessel was not there, and they were afraid to go without him. The Captain said that was no matter; and told me to go up, and cast off the fast. He ordered the men on deck, and to make sail directly — They obeyed quietly. It was a bright night, and we had a good wind—arrived safe at Bangor, and paid them well for their trouble. We then made the best of our way towards Dublin. On the second night, we managed to get into the upper loft of a stable before it was shut up—having previously made an examination of the horses. When every thing was quiet, we came down, and found two men asleep, with a lantern burning near them. We called to them in a low voice, and they awoke. We presented our pistols, and the Captain told them if they said a word, they should die on the spot. One of them was very much alarmed; and the Captain told me to take care of him. I fastened him to one of the stalls, and tied up his mouth with his handkerchief. We made the other put on saddles and bridles to the two best horses in the stable; tied him in the same manner as the other; gave each of them a guinea, and moved off.

In three days we reached Dublin, taking the by-roads, and robbing nobody. We went to the inn where I had been so much acquainted, when I lived in D. The landlord was glad to see me, and had no suspicions that I was a bad fellow. I told him that I had been living at Kilkenny, ever since I left D. and was in very good business. He told me that the Lord Mayor's girl was married, and lived near his house; but I was afraid to go near her.—He laughed about the trick I had played upon her, and said that she had been very near dying, in consequence of hanging up to dry there all night. We staid at this house for four days, and paid him well, not to let any one know that we were there. In the day time we kept quiet; but at night we would go round the city, in search of game. We found some *good pickings* in this line, and shared about 140 pounds each; the greater part of which, we buried in a grove, out of the city. On the fifth day, as I was walking alone, by the Bank of Ireland, I saw an extra stage for Kilkenny, standing near the bank, and two or three packages brought out and put into the stage— which I supposed were of some value. I went back to Doherty immediately, and gave him the information—I proposed to go out and overtake the stage, and we should probably, make a *grand haul*.

He objected, saying that it was too hazardous an experiment, particularly in the day time—That there were, no doubt, many passengers, as also many travellers on the road. He refused so obstinately, and my mind was so much set upon it, that I determined to set out alone. I set off on foot, and came up with the stage about four miles from the city. There were not many people passing on the road, but the stage was full of passengers. I watched the opportunity, and as the back of the stage was closed, had no difficulty in cutting the straps which bound on the trunks behind. There was a leather covering over them, which I also cut, and pulled out one trunk—dropped it in the road; kept hold of the stage, and a little further on pulled out another, and so on, until I had got off four of them. I then went back and collected all of them; carried them into a field, and with my master-key, opened all of them. I was much disappointed in the receipts of this adventure—for out of these four trunks, I only gathered about nine pounds, in gold, silver and paper. They were principally filled with ladies' and gentlemen's clothes and papers. I selected a genteel dress, and put it in a bundle. I then hung out a red handkerchief on a tree, and distributed the clothes and goods about. I wrote an advertisement, and posted it up on the tree, that those goods were to be sold the next day at public auction. I moved off over the fields, with my bundle on my back, and passed for a pedlar. I came to a large house, and a surly looking man was standing at the gate, who appeared to be the owner. I asked him if he would give me some beer—he said I might go to the next ale house and buy it. I then asked him what auction that was, which was to be in yonder field tomorrow. He said he had not heard of any, I told him what I had seen, and he did not believe me—at length I told him I would shew him. He called one of his servants, and we went along. He was in a great passion when he saw the fact, and swore a great deal about the impudence of any person in advertising such an auction on his grounds, without his consent. He then, in great anger, began to throw the goods into the street. I saw a number of people coming down the road, upon a full drive, and thought it best to get out of their reach. I left him at work, and made the best of my way to Dublin. Some days after I had been there, I saw a servant of this man, who told me that a number of people had come back from the first tavern, where the stage had stopped, in pursuit of the trunks. Seeing them lying in the road, and the owner of the grounds busy in examining the clothes, &c. they asked him his name, and told him to deliver up the money, and all the contents of the trunks. They quarrelled; and at last, the people took this man into custody, tied him neck and heels, and carried him off for examination, as the robber. The magistrate before whom he was taken, knew him, and was satisfied that there must be some mistake. He immediately discharged him, and he told them the whole story about my coming to him, which caused them to set out in pursuit of me. I remained concealed in Dublin, for some days. When I came there, my first inquiry was for the Captain—The landlord told me that he had gone out, and would soon be back. I went in pursuit of him, but he did not return that night.

I never saw John Doherty from this time. Since I have been in America, I received a letter from him, informing me, that he had found out my departure from Ireland for New-York, the day after the vessel sailed; that he had scoured the country for some weeks after; and being pressed very close, he had gathered up his treasures, and pushed off to one of the West India Islands, where he was comfortably settled; and under a fictitious name, transacting much business, in an honest manner. He directed to me in the name that I had agreed to take, in case of separation. It was sent to the care of the British Consul, who advertised the letter, and I sent for it. This man had a great many good qualities; and although he was the cause of much trouble to me, yet I feel a strong affection for him; and trust that he will die a repentant and honest man.

After searching in vain for the Captain, I went to Donnybrook-Fair, in the neighborhood of the city, and spent a great deal of money, in carousing and gambling. I entered into all the sports which are usual in that place of festivity and mirth. I saw a jaunting car and horse standing in the yard of an inn; ordered the ostler to bring out my horse, which he did—I put two girls in it, and drove off as boldly as if it was my own. We travelled round the country, for four days, until we had got tired of each other's company. I put them into a stage for Dublin, and bid them good-bye. I then sold the horse and car, and walked back to Dublin; robbing only one person on the road, of a small sum in paper, and a diamond breast-pin.

I went to visit an old friend and relation of mine, who was a gardener, in the service of the Lord-Lieutenant. I saw a servant girl there who was very pretty, and I spent the greater part of my time there for five days. I had then become quite intimate with her, and wished to stay all night. She objected, saying that the Lord-Lieutenant would find it out—that he had a machine, by which he could see into any room in the house, by holding it to the key hole. I did not believe it; and as she was so much afraid of this machine, I was anxious to see it, and get it away from him if possible. She described it as an elegant gold snuff-box, the top of which was covered with diamonds. I found out that he used to walk early in the morning, near a fish pond at the extremity of his garden, and I immediately determined to put him under contribution. The next two mornings were rainy, and he did not go out; but on the third morning, through the assistance of my friend, the gardener, I had access to the garden, and took my post early in the morning. About nine o'clock, I saw his excellency approaching, with one servant walking after him—no other people were in sight. I concealed myself under the boughs of some laurel trees near the pond, waiting for the servant to separate. The Lord-Lieutenant had a large gold headed cane in his hand; and in a few minutes he sat down on a bench, on the margin of the pond. The servant went round the other side, into some shrubbery; and I then came out of my hiding place, went boldly up to the master, presented my large double-barrelled pistol, and demanded all the money he had about him. He looked at me for a few moments, and then said, "Did you speak to me?" "Yes, your honor." "What do you want, you impudent rascal," said he, "get out of my presence, or I will have your skin taken off." "Please your honor," said I, "I must first skin your pockets; and if you offer to call for assistance, and do not give over immediately, I shall take your life." He seeing me so resolute, gave up his purse, which was a pretty rich haul. He was then about moving—I told him to wait a little while longer, that I had not half done with him. I then ordered him to hand out his watch, and the ring upon his finger. He hesitated for some time, and begged me not to take them from him, for they were worth more to him than their real value in money. I said they are so much the more valuable to me. He offered to deposit any sum of money, in any private place that I should name, if I would let him retain them. I said, "you don't suppose that I should be fool enough to go after it, and be detected by your soldiers." At last, however, I allowed him to keep the ring, and was upon the point of leaving him—"As your honor," said I, "has been so obliging, will you just be kind enough to give me a pinch of snuff." He immediately pulled out his diamond snuff box! and as soon as he opened it, I snatched it out of his hand, and put it in my pocket. I then told him that I had *milked* him well enough, and that, if he talked loud about it, I should visit him again. He told me he was sorry that such a likely young man as I appeared to be, should be a robber; and advised me to do so no more. I answered, that it was my trade; and that I only took what his countrymen had robbed from the poor Irish. He asked me my name—I said, "Captain Lightfoot, at your service." "Ah, says he—where is your comrade, the notorious Thunderbolt?" "He is gone out on business; but if you say much about this affair, I shall request him to take supper with you this evening." He pressed me to go into the house, and get some spirits; but I of course declined. I saw some people at a distance, and retreated backwards, still holding my pistol towards him. I reached a part of the garden wall, which I thought I could scale easily, and just as I had mounted it, he gave the alarm. All the servants bawled aloud, and I had just time to get round the corner of the first street. I walked slowly, and on looking round, saw nobody in pursuit, I then quickened my pace, and stopped not until I had reached the circular road. I swam the Liffey, at Chapel Izard. The weather was quite cold, and as I was wet through, I stopped at a small house, where I dried my clothes and got some refreshment. I remained till night, when I started for Kilkenny on foot—kept out of the public road, and reached Kilkenny in four days. I went to a cousin's house, and remained until I found that there was a large reward offered for my detection —describing my person exactly. They probably found out my real name from the gardener, who was my relation, for I saw him when I was scaling the wall. I staid but two nights at Kilkenny; and seeing an advertisement of a vessel at Waterford, that was to sail immediately for New-York, I started off to take passage in her. That night I buried the extra watches, and all the money which I did not immediately want—sewed up the rest in the waistband of my pantaloons, and changed my dress to the most shabby and ragged one that I could find—I painted my face, put a bandage on one knee, and a pack of old clothes on my back. I walked in this manner for one day, and at night went into a stable and borrowed a horse, which carried me very comfortably to Waterford.

I immediately entered my name as a passenger in the brig Maria, Captain Condin, which was bound direct to New-York, and was appointed to sail the next day. I called myself then, Michael O'Hanlan.

On the 12th of April, 1819, I went on board, having kept myself concealed till that time. The vessel had dropped down the harbor, and was all ready, waiting for me and five others. As soon as we came on board, she got under way, with a fine stiff breeze; and "then, I wouldn't call the King of England my brother." There were about 120 passengers, men, women and children, on board. We had very rough weather, particularly when approaching the coast of America—Our provisions and water were nearly exhausted, and we were all put upon short allowance. The captain said he should put into the first port; and one morning said that he should go into St. John's (New Brunswick,) or Halifax. I did not like this plan; for I did not wish to go into any of the British dominions. So I excited some ten or twelve of the crew who were anxious to go to the United States, to assist me, and we would force the captain to go there. The mate was an American, and a clever fellow; and although he did not wish to interfere, we plainly found that he would assist

The Mutiny on Board the Brig "Maria"

us. He told us from day to day the latitude and longitude, and said that we might easily get to some port in the United States. We had made a complete mutiny, and a committee went to the captain, desiring him to steer for the first port in the United States. He swore he would not; that he would put into St. John's or Halifax. We remonstrated, and insisted that he had agreed to carry us to New-York, and that we might reach there, or some northern port, without much difficulty. He went down in the cabin with his son, and they came up on deck, both armed—He ordered us below, and we then threatened to take command of the vessel. He cocked his pistol—I immediately sprung at him, seized him by the throat, and took his pistol from him. His son was coming at me, and I knocked him down. Some of the crew came up to rescue the captain, and there was a general engagement for a few minutes. I said, unless he would agree to make the first port in the United States, we would put the mate in command of the brig, and confine him below. He at last consented; and we arrived in Salem, on the 17th of June, 1819.

Many of the passengers were sick, and some of them had died on the passage. In consequence of this, the vessel was detained at quarantine. I was perfectly well, and was anxious to come on shore, as were most of the other passengers. They placed a guard on board to prevent this. Among the sol-

diers that came from the fort, was one or two of
my countrymen — We conversed in Irish; and
they agreed to help some of us to get off. They
came in a boat one night, and we prepared to go,
but the guard discovered us. The boat was along
side, and I advanced first to the gangway. The
guard stopped me, and I knocked him down without ceremony. The soldiers were then afraid to
take us, and rowed off; so that we were obliged to
stay, until we were suffered to come up to town.
At Salem, I saw a number of gentlemen who
wished to hire servants, or laborers. I pretended
to be foolish, spoke only in Irish, and looked as
silly as I could. Some of them were engaged as
laborers, and some of them went off to New-York.
I remained in Salem, frolicing and carousing, until I had spent all my money. I had a companion,
James Manny, and when his money was all gone,
we began to look about for work. It was many
days before we could get any employment—The
people did not like our appearance. They asked
me if I could reap or sow, or dig—I said "no, but
I was a good farmer." This was the first *bull* that
I made in America. We at last, went to E. H.
Derby, Esq. who agreed to take us on trial. We
went to work, making hay—James was not fit for
any thing, and staid only a week—got sick, and
at last, was obliged to be sent to the poor-house.
I worked very willingly, for some time, and very
industriously—I remained with Mr. Derby about

COURT STREET, SALEM, MASSACHUSETTS

At the left of the Court House in the middle of the street, is the three
story house in which lived E. H. Derby, Esq.

fourteen months—during which time, I labored harder than I ever did before in my life. I believe Mr. D. was generally satisfied with me; but I would sometimes get drunk, and neglect my work. Whenever I received any money, I would go to Salem, and have a great blow out, and then would be very inattentive and quarrelsome. After having given me many warnings, Mr. D. was compelled to dismiss me. During my stay there, I was treated with much kindness and attention by Mr. Derby and his family; and might have remained there, honestly and quietly, if it had not been for my disposition to intemperance and riot. I never stole any thing while I was there, nor wronged Mr. Derby of a sixpence. When I left him, I wandered about, until I had squandered away all my money; and not being able to get employment, I tried to get back to Ireland, but had no means of paying for my passage.

During my residence in Salem, I came to Boston only once—This was on Sunday, and I went to the Catholic Church, which was the only time I went into a church while I was in America. I had habitually neglected this duty in my own country; and although born a Roman Catholic, I had never been a member of that communion, having not been confirmed.

When I went to Mr. Derby's, I pretended to be very ignorant, and that I could neither read nor write. One day when I was working in the field, he brought me a letter from Ireland, directed to his care. I opened it, and immediately burst out with an exclamation of true sorrow, saying that my father was dead. I had written a letter to my father in Ireland, soon after I had engaged myself with Mr. D.; stating my situation, my repentance for the crimes which forced me to leave Ireland, and my determination to lead an honest life. This letter was from one of my brothers, and Mr. D. was astonished that I should understand it, as he had always supposed that I could not write nor read. He asked me to account for this, and why I should have known so quickly after opening the letter, that my father was dead. I made some excuse for it, which satisfied him at the time—I forget what it was—Perhaps it was the black seal. However, he read the letter, and was convinced of the fact.

After leaving Mr. Derby's, I roved about in dissipation and idleness, for some weeks, when I found that it was necessary to attempt some means to get a decent living. I might then have taken to my old trade of robbery; but I had made up my mind to be as honest as I could. I engaged myself to a brewer in Salem, and worked tolerably well for a few weeks—having no other vices to reproach myself with, during this time, than intemperance and gambling. When I left the brewery, through the advice of some of my countrymen, I went to Portsmouth, (N. H.) and loitered

A Portsmouth Gin Shop

about there some weeks, without any business.
While there, an Irishman at Salem, wrote me that
a letter had come from home for me, in the charge
of a Captain Wilson, which probably, contained
a sum of money. I went to Salem, and obtained
the letter—It was from my eldest brother, who
was executor of my father's estate; and he en-
closed me a bill of exchange for about 400 dollars, which sum my father had bequeathed to me.
I received the money for the bill; returned to
Portsmouth; and after spending a week or more,
in dissipation and gambling, I concluded to embark in some business. I had then more than five
hundred dollars in money—I heard there was a
small brewery vacant, belonging to ——— Adams,
Esq. which had recently been occupied by Peter
King. I took a lease of the whole establishment,
and determined to go to work industriously. I
hired my workmen—put the house in repair, and
paid cash for the grain, &c. necessary to begin the
business. All that winter and spring, I carried on
the trade industriously. I sold considerable quan-
tities of beer and porter, and might have made
money out of it, if I had known enough of the people with whom I had to deal—But they were too
sharp for me; and I grew dissatisfied—returned
to my old habits of intemperance, and got myself
involved in debt. My property was attached, and
I owed more than I was able to pay. It was in May,
1821, when I failed. I had made many bad debts,

and I tried in vain to collect them; but still I had reserved money enough to save me from immediate distress.

After idling about for a fortnight, I went to Mr. Stacy Hall, to hire a horse and chaise, for the purpose of going about the country, to collect what was due me. He had no hesitation in accommodating me, for my character was not so bad in Portsmouth as to make him suspicious. I travelled about all that day, and could not collect more than about sixty dollars. At night I came to Greenland, to pay a visit to a young girl with whom I had been very intimate, and who I had promised to marry.

I remained with her till midnight. I told her frankly my situation—that I was not able to marry her, but proposed to her that she should go to Canada with me—that I had money enough to bear expenses there, and that I had many friends and relations in the neighborhood of Montreal. I told her that I could no doubt, get into business there, and then we would live happily together for life. But all my entreaties would not prevail —she would not elope from her friends; and I set off for Canada about midnight. I travelled as fast as possible. There were no incidents worth recording, on this journey. For the sake of keeping my hand in, I lifted about seventy dollars in Vermont, from a Connecticut pedlar. He tried to resist me, and I knocked him from his cart. I took

it for granted, that he had been cheating some innocent people out of this money, and that it would
be much better in my keeping than in his. With
this exception, I did not attempt to rob any one, or
to stop at any place longer than was necessary, until I reached Quebec. This was in the beginning
of June last.

I went to a respectable tavern in Quebec, called
myself Joseph Hendley, and as I was well dressed,
I suppose I passed for a gentleman. The chaise
which I had brought with me, I sold for £20,
Canada currency—a few days after, sold the horse
at auction, for sixty three dollars. I then bought
a suit of quaker's clothes, of the first quality, and
a large broad brimmed hat. The first day I came
to Quebec, I purchased a sword-cane — I had
brought with me two pistols, one of which I had
got in Portsmouth, and the other was the old
friend I had used in Ireland. I had a plenty of
money, knew nobody in Canada, and cared for
nobody. I remained about ten days in Quebec;
during which time, I had made all proper inquiries about the roads and distances. After paying
my bill at the tavern, and as soon as my new dress
was completed, I started from Quebec early in
the evening, with my bundle in my hand. After
travelling a few miles, I put on the quaker clothes,
and faced for the Three Rivers. The next day I
found the heat rather uncomfortable, and my
clothes too tight; but my hat was of good service

to keep off the sun. That night, I lodged at the house of a Frenchman, and was so kindly treated, that I would not attempt any robbery from him. I was quite sick, from the fatigue of the day, and his family paid every attention to me. I remained here two days, and then set out on my journey. In the forenoon of the next day, being then about 25 miles from Quebec, I met two well dressed gentlemen, in a calash, riding slowly. I halted in the road, when they came up, and reined in their horse. I said, "will thee please to give me the time of day?" I had previously put the chain of my watch out of sight. One of these men spoke broken English; but the one nearest me, seemed to be an Irishman. This one immediately pulled out an elegant gold watch. I drew my large pistol, cocked it, and told him to give it up to me instantly. He did so. I then said to the other, you must deliver up your watch and money. He seemed frightened—muttered in broken English, and pretended not to understand me. I then snatched the reins out of the hands of the other, and said, violently, "you will both lose your lives unless you shell out directly." They talked a few moments in French, and then seeing me so determined, they handed over their pocket books and purses. The Frenchman's watch was an old silver one—I told him he might have that, for it was not worth the trouble of carrying about. I then gave back the reins, and bid them good bye.

The amount I received this time, was about 40 dollars in paper, and about 20 in specie. They drove away fast, and as soon as they were out of sight, I turned out of the road into the fields— stopped at a small house, for some refreshment, and inquired about the roads, and then pushed into the woods, where I slept all night. In the morning I crossed over again, into the Three Rivers road, and travelled as fast as possible all that day, without attempting to stop any one. Towards evening I met an old gentleman on horseback. I told him in a loud voice, to stop—presented the pistol to his breast, and said, " give me up every dollar you have about you." He gave me his pocket book, in great terror. I examined it hastily, and took out about thirty five dollars in paper, and then returned it to him. That night I went into a small house, out of the road, where I remained quiet, pretending to be sick, all the next day and night.

I had not proceeded far the next day, when I met a young Frenchman, on a handsome bay horse. I drew my sword, and told him I should run him through, if he did not give up his money. He took out an old pocket book—it contained about three dollars; which I said was not enough for my purpose. I dropped my sword-cane and bundle, pulled out a pistol, and told him to dismount. He hesitated—saying that the horse was a borrowed one, and he should lose his character, if he did not return it. I told him, that I wanted to borrow it too; and that it was better for him to lose his character than his life. He turned his horse's head, and was going off—I fired my pistol over him, without any intention of shooting him, or hurting the horse. He imagined himself killed, and fell from the horse—I ran after him, and snatched the bridle out of his hand—He soon recovered from his fright, and begged for his life. I told him not to be alarmed, that I only wanted to take a short ride on his horse—he might have him again in a few days. I then told him to go back for my bundle and cane. When he came with them, I demanded his spurs—He took them off, and put them on my feet—I tied my bundle to the saddle—gave the poor fellow a dollar for his trouble, and rode off with all speed.

In the day time, I laid by, at a small hut, and at night took the main road. The horse was a good one, and I made him travel rapidly. The next day after this last affair, I went into the woods, and took off my quaker clothes, and put them into a small portmanteau, which I had bought in the morning, from a farmer. I heard of many inquiries about a quaker, and saw many people in pursuit of him; but as my other clothes made me look so much like a gentleman, there was no suspicion of me. I took the road to Montreal, and generally travelled at night—resting in the day time, at small huts, out of the public road.

I arrived at Montreal, and put up at the Mansion-house, where I passed for a gentleman, and staid there eight days—which time was spent in dissipation and intemperance. I had no chance to take any thing, although I made many attempts. I inquired the way to Kingston, Upper Canada, and set out early in the morning, having paid a large bill at the tavern. I stopped at an Indian village, called Cogunawognah, about 15 miles from Montreal, where I remained that night. Although I could not understand either Indian or French, I was hospitably received, and remained there for two days. After riding about 20 miles on the road to Kingston, I met with an Indian Chief, alone in a calash—He was well dressed, and had many ornaments about him, of gold and silver. I rode up to him, presented a pistol, and told him to stop instantly. He hesitated, and made a grasp at the pistol—I snatched the reins out of his hand, and cocked my pistol, saying that I would kill him on the spot, if he did not deliver up all his money. He took off his ornaments, and gave me about $65 in specie and paper. He then said, if I would throw down my pistol, he would fight me, and he could easily get back his money. I tried to make him understand that it was not my way of fighting—That in my country, we made use of the shillelah. He understood this word; and immediately said, "ah! you Irishman then?—I fight you so." I told him, if he would wait till I went into the woods, and cut a stick, I would throw away my pistol, and fight him—He agreed. I pushed off into the bushes, and put the spurs to my horse. He suspected that I was trying to get away from him, and he got out of the calash and pursued me. He ran nearly as fast as my horse; set up the Indian halloo, and in a few moments, there were as many as twenty Indians in pursuit of me. However, I outran them, and came to a river, where the current was too rapid for me to cross. While I was resting on the bank, I saw the Indian coming through the woods—He came up to me before I had time to mount my horse. He had a large stone in his hand, which he threw at me with great violence, and then stooped to pick up another. I thought there might be more Indians behind, and for the preservation of my own life, I thought I was justified in taking his. As he approached, I fired my pistol, and he fell. This is the only time in my life, that I ever intended to take the life of a fellow being. I am afraid that I killed him; but yet I trust, that he was only wounded.

I did not wait long, but set off with full speed. I kept my course by the banks of the river, and did not discover that I was pursued. I met with some Indians, who were very civil to me, and gave me some provisions. I came to St. John's, without any interruption, and rested for two days. From thence I went to Isle Noir. On my way there, I met a poor woman in a small cabin, who solicited charity—I gave her all the money I could spare; and she directed me to Isle Noir. I staid there a few days; but found there was nothing of any consequence to be had, and that I was no safer there, than in Montreal. I then returned, with an intention of going to Kingston, for I was apprehensive that I should be pursued. I carried with me a bottle of liquor and some provisions, as also a bag of corn for the horse. I was two days in the woods, without meeting with any human creature except an old Indian, who gave me the proper direction for Kingston. Soon after I had got out of the woods, I stopped at a small tavern and rested, for my horse was almost tired out. In the evening, a blustering fellow, in the King's uniform, came to the house on horseback—He behaved so impertinently, that I was determined to have a cut at him. I asked him the road to Kingston; and his answer was, "get out, you vagabond —how dare you be so familiar with his Majesty's officers?" I was disgusted with this man's conduct. We were alone, in the room of a tavern, and my only object was to have some innocent conversation with him; not expecting to be treated so contemptuously. To be sure, my appearance might have been against me—My beard was long, and my clothes much soiled, but not ragged. I found out from the landlord, that this fellow was going about four miles further that night; and I went off on foot in the direction he was to take. When he came up, it was after dark. I cried out, stop! in a loud voice. He obeyed—I went up, seized the reins of his horse, presented my pistol, and said, "Mr. Lobster, get off directly." He trembled and dismounted. I told him to give up all his money. He had only a small quantity of specie, which I took, and threw away. He begged for his life. There was a pistol in his holster; I asked him why he did not defend himself with that. He said very humbly, that he never fired at gentlemen; and again begged that I would spare his life. I ordered him to take off his coat and cap, which he did instantly; still begging me not to hurt him. I then told him to tie the horse to a tree, by the side of the road. I took off his cravat, and with that and his pocket handkerchief, I tied his hands behind him, and fastened him to a tree; telling him that I was the person he had behaved so uncivilly to, at the tavern, and that this was the reward for him. I told him if he opened his mouth, till I was out of sight, I should come back and blow his brains out. He promised to be quiet, and I mounted his horse and rode off, leaving my own in the stable. As mine was almost worn down by hard riding, I thought I should get on better with his. I rode all that night. At the first stream of water I came to, I took the red coat, put some stones in it, and sunk it.

After riding for two days, and stopping only for refreshment, I had lost my way. I met no person that morning, on the road, and saw no house

where I could get any information. At last, I overtook a man on horseback, and although he looked
like a gentleman, I rather chose to find out the
road, than to rob him. I accosted him politely,
and he gave me all necessary information. We
rode on in company, for a few miles, and having
received his instructions, I arrived at Kingston. I
remained here four days, at a respectable inn; and
having brushed up a little, I passed without suspicion. Once or twice, I tried to start some game,
but without success; so that I thought it best to
go back again to Montreal, which was about 150
miles distant. On the second night, I stopped at a
decent farmer's house, to rest, because I had rode
all the night before, and I wished to give the horse
some good food. In the course of the evening, I
asked the farmer if there was any land for sale in
the neighborhood, and pretended that I wanted to
purchase some. He said there was an old gentleman lived about five miles off, who was very rich,
and owned large tracts of land. In the morning
he directed me to the house. I found an old gentleman and his son in the parlor. I told him that
I had lately come over from England, with a
number of emigrants, and that I wished to purchase a good tract of land. We conversed for two
or three hours, most of which time he was describing the lands that he had for sale. He shewed
me about his grounds, house, &c. I found out that
his men were all to work in the fields, and that

only his son and himself were near the house. His son we left writing in the parlor; and when he had taken me into an upper room, to shew me the fine prospect in the rear of his house, I drew my pistol, and said I should take his life, unless he told me where his money was. He said he had no money, but what was in a small purse, which he handed me. I told him I did not believe him, and was so resolute with him, that he at last said he had some in a desk, in the next room to that one where his son was. I then told him to lay down on the bed, and not to speak a word. He was so frightened that he obeyed instantly. I tore the sheet into small strips, bound his arms and legs, and put a bandage over his mouth. I then locked him in, and went down stairs, to the son. I walked about very deliberately for some time, and told the son that I was waiting for his father, who was out in the stable. I requested him to order my horse, and after he had called some time for a servant, he went out himself to bring the horse to the door. In the mean time, I went into the other room, opened an old desk with my master-key, and took out a bag, which, I found afterwards, contained about £170 in gold and silver. I had some trouble in getting all of this into my different pockets, before the son brought the horse. When he came, I told him that I was going a few miles, for an attorney to make the deeds, and should return in the afternoon. I told him his father had just gone up stairs, and wished to see him. I immediately mounted my horse, and *cleared out like a white head.*

I then rode into the woods, changed my dress, and put on my quaker clothes. On the road to Montreal, I met with no impediment, although I saw many advertisements, describing my person and horse. One day I fell in with a company of men, women, and children, who proved to be emigrants from Ireland, and were going to Kingston, as settlers, or employment as laborers. They were travelling on foot, and appeared to be in great distress. I conversed with them for some time, and found that one or two of them had come from my part of the country, and had heard of me and my family. In the course of my inquiries, they answered that Captain Lightfoot was hanged in Dublin; and that they were happy that his poor father and mother did not live to see him come to such an end. I did not discover myself; but giving them all the money I could spare, I separated from them, and came to Montreal again, without any molestation. I remained here but two days. On the second night, I was in company with a number of high fellows, some of whom were *black legs.* I shewed a quantity of money, and they were very anxious that I should play cards with them. We set down, and I was loser for some time, because I did not understand the game; but in the course of the night, I found out a way of cheating, so that when they had lost all their money, I had won upwards of 200 dollars of them. I told them I must go to bed, and we would play again tomorrow. I said that I did not want their money, and that I would treat them handsomely. I called the landlord, and ordered the best dinner that he could provide, for the next day, and requested them to invite all their friends. When they had all retired, I paid my bill, and ordered my horse, intending to get out of their company as soon as possible. My intention was to come back again to the States, and I took the road to Lake Champlain. I threw aside the quaker dress, and gave it to an old woman, on the road, who furnished me with supper, and a safe lodging for the night. At almost every tavern, I saw advertisements after me, and heard of people who were in pursuit, from Kingston—so I made as little delay as possible. I buried all the money that I had no use for, and three watches. I had already left a considerable sum in possession of some friends at Montreal. I then crossed over to Grand Isle, on the American side, where I remained for three days. I was standing at the door of the tavern one forenoon, and a man drove up with some advertisements in his hand. He asked me if I was the tavern keeper—I said yes. He then handed me one of the advertisements, and requested me to have it posted up. He said it was for the apprehension of one of the most notorious rascals that had ever been known. I invited him to come in and get something to drink. I told him that I had been robbed myself, by that man, and that I would add twenty pounds in addition to the reward for his detection. I asked him how many hand-bills he had. He said about fifty; and that he was going to Vermont to circulate them, for he had been informed that the rascal had gone that way. I told him that I had intended to set out the next day, in pursuit of him; and that I would take the hand-bills, and distribute them myself, about the country. He readily gave me up all his advertisements, and went back, much obliged to me for taking the trouble off his hands.

I crossed over to Burlington with my horse, as soon as I could get a conveyance, having first destroyed all the advertisements. I put up my horse at a large tavern in Burlington; and as I was going to bed, I saw an advertisement, describing my person exactly, and there were one or two people in the bar-room watching me very closely. I walked about the room very quietly, for a few moments, and then went slowly out of the back door. As soon as I ascertained that no one was following me, I took to my heels, through the woods, and did not stop until I had ran for the space of an hour and a half. I judged it most prudent to leave my horse behind me. I avoided public roads as much as possible, keeping near enough only, that I should not lose my way. I kept out of the road when I saw any one approaching; and by sleeping in barns and eating in obscure houses, I arrived at Enfield, in New Hampshire, without detection. Here I began to recover my courage, and determined to walk no more, if I could get well mounted. I moved on, towards Concord, which was considered the most public road, and kept a bright look out for a good horse. I watched day and night, for some time, at the small taverns, but found nothing that was worth my acceptance—" The horses were as lean as the owners' purses." I went about the small villages, to see if I could *hook* any thing, and then determined to go to Boston, where I had no doubt I could get something; and if I did not succeed, I could probably find an opportunity of embarking for the West Indies, to meet my old friend Thunderbolt.

I was upon the look out for a horse, and had money enough even to buy one. On Thursday afternoon, in the beginning of August, I went into a farm house for refreshment—I got something to eat. They said the name of the town was Boscawen, and gave me directions for Boston. I remained until it was evening, and then set out on the road to Concord. It was a fine moonlight night; and about eleven o'clock, I heard the tread of a horse behind me—I got into the bushes, and lay concealed. In a few minutes, two men came up slowly on horseback. It was so light that one of them discovered me as I was crawling down in bushes. He stopped, and the other rode on. The man looked for some time, and then drew closer. I remained still. At length he cried, "who's there?" once or twice. I made him no answer. He then said, "you must tell who you are." I stood up, and drew my pistol, and said I would let him know who I was—"I am the bold Doherty, from Scotland." "And what are you there after," said he. "If you'll stop a moment, I'll tell you;" and then advanced close to him, presented my pistol, and told him to give me his money, or I would have his life. He gave me all the money, together with his pocket-book and papers. I then ordered him to dismount; that I wanted to see what money he had under the saddle. He was very much agitated when he got off, and begged hard for his life. I told him that I should not hurt him, but that he must keep out of the way. I ordered him to stand back by the fence, and not open his mouth. He obeyed instantly, and I cried, "John, take care of this fellow," to make him think that I had some comrade in the rear. He was a stout fellow, and if he had shewn spirit enough, might have given me a good battle. He had a pretty good horse, with a brown surtout and a small bundle tied to the saddle. His name, I afterwards found by the advertisement, was Karr. I mounted, bade him good night, and rode off. I did not make much stay in any place, till I reached Londonderry, where I stopped some time to refresh myself. On

Friday morning, I overtook a man on horseback. I inquired where he was going—he said to Newburyport. I observed that I was going the same way, and should be glad to keep company with him. We jogged along together for some miles, and stopped once to drink. The conversation turned upon the robbery at Boscawen. I said it was a most daring thing, and wished I could detect the robber. I expressed my fears at travelling alone, particularly as I had some money about me. He said he would be afraid to travel at night— that he had been up the country, to collect money for a man in Portsmouth; and although he had a pistol with him, he should not consider himself safe, for he had heard that there was a gang of fifty of these fellows around the country. We agreed to stand by each other, if we were attacked. He asked me my name, and I told him it was Morrison—that I belonged to Londonderry; and as there were so many Irish there, he readily believed me.

When we had reached a small brook, we stopped to let our horses drink. I then pulled out a pistol and held it close to his head, and demanded that he should give up that money he had been at so much trouble to collect. He asked what I meant. I replied, "do you not remember the business at Boscawen?" He trembled, and begged for his life. I told him that it was only his money that was of any use to me. He handed over his pocket book, which contained upwards of one hundred dollars. I told him that if he attempted to follow, or make an alarm, I should surely shoot him. He promised

NEWBURYPORT FROM THE SALISBURY SIDE OF THE RIVER

not to, and I rode off. As soon as I was out of sight of him, I crossed over the fields, and lay concealed for some time in the woods; then inquired the way to Newburyport; took the cross roads, and that night arrived at Salisbury. I was afraid to go into any tavern or large house, so I turned the horse out in a field, and went into an old hut, where I rested myself for a few hours. At day break I started, and had some difficulty in catching my

horse. I was fatigued, riding so much on horseback, and thought I would look round and pick up
a good chaise. Near Salisbury meeting house, I
saw four or five good chaises; one or two of them
had harnesses. It was scarcely day break, and no
people were stirring—So I took the chaise, and
brought it about half a mile, to the field where I
had left the horse. I harnessed him to the chaise,
and tied my saddle behind it. I then took a roundabout road, and reached Newburyport about noon.
I went to the stage tavern, had my horse taken
care of, and ordered a good dinner. I heard some
talk about the Boscawen robbery; but nobody
seemed to suspect me. The landlord knew me
when I was a brewer, in Portsmouth, and believed
that I had just come from there. In the evening I
walked out, and found a girl that I had been acquainted with in Salem, and agreed to meet her at
nine o'clock. I returned to the tavern, got my supper, and then went with the bar-keeper to a lec-
ture. I staid a few minutes in the meeting house,
and then slipped out, unknown to him. I walked
about near the wharves, and in a narrow street or
passage way, met a well dressed man. I accosted
him very politely, and asked him if he would be
good enough to tell me what o'clock it was. He
hesitated some time, and then said, "what the
devil do you ask such questions for; did you not
just hear the clock strike?" "Yes," said I; "but
I want to hear your watch strike, or I shall strike

your head"—At the same time holding a pistol close to him. He gave me a watch, and a small pocket book, containing about forty dollars in bank bills.* I then returned as rapidly as possible to the tavern; ordered the boy to put my horse to the chaise, and paid my bill. I said to the landlord, that it was so pleasant an evening, I wanted to take a small ride round the town. I then called for the girl, and she agreed to go to Salem with me. I gave her the watch I had lifted from the man, that evening; having taken off the chain. We set off for Salem, taking the old road— Stopped some time at the tavern in Ipswich, where I heard much conversation about the Boscawen robbery; so I thought it was not prudent to stay any longer, and drove off again. We reached a small tavern, near Beverly, late that night, and went to bed. Early in the morning, I told the girl that I had business to do in Boston, and would be

* Since the publication of the first edition, an obscure newspaper, at Newburyport, has attempted to disprove this anecdote, and to call in question the verity of the whole narration, because the robbery here alluded to, was never heard of in that town. The truth is, that many discerning men in Newburyport, are satisfied from other circumstances, that this is true, and have no difficulty in designating the man who was robbed. It would add nothing to the interest of this pamphlet, if his name were mentioned. The man is said to be a great bully; and as he prides himself upon his prowess, he would not be very anxious to promulgate the story of his own disgrace, and to tell the good people of that town, that he was robbed, and vanquished in a personal rencontre, by a smaller man than himself. Besides, no man, however creditable, would, in that section of the country, since the notorious mock robbery of Major Goodridge, expect to gain belief, unless he could produce other evidence of the fact, than his own assertion. At any rate, there is nothing more remarkable in this particular robbery, than in some of those which are detailed, and can be verified. It is Martin's dying relation, and every reader is at full liberty, to give as much faith as he pleases, to this, or any other fact here recorded.

absent but three days, and hoped she would remain there until I returned. I gave her about fifty dollars, and deposited some with the landlord for her expenses in my absence. I then drove to Danvers, where I got breakfast. I had some acquaintances who worked in Crowninshield's factory, and I staid with them some time; this was on a Sunday morning. I left the chaise there, and saddled the horse. My friends agreed to meet me in Salem, and have a good blow out—We spent the day and night, drinking and carousing—all at my expense. I had some clothes in Salem, and I changed my dress there. After breakfast, I left them, and started for Boston, where I arrived about 12 o'clock. I found out some of my countrymen, in Broad Street, and walked about the town with them. I went on to the Common to see the military parade; but found too many people there for my business. I returned to the Sun Tavern, near Broad Street, where I dined.

In the afternoon, I mounted the horse, and rode out to take a view of the country, and to find out what was going on out of town. I had understood that there was to be a large party at the Governor's, to dinner, and thought of course, there might be some *fat ones* among them; and "I thought I would make one among the company." I went over Cragie's bridge, and at the tavern, found out the road to Medford. On the way there, I fell in with a countryman of mine, that I had known in Salem, and invited him to drink with me. We went into a store, where we drank considerably. He soon separated from me, saying he

BEVERLY AND THE ESSEX BRIDGE TO SALEM

must go to Boston. This man had no knowledge whatever of my intentions, and is, for aught I know, an honest fellow. I offered to sell my horse to the man who kept the store, as he was much fatigued, and of very little use to me. He seemed to doubt whether it was my property, and hesitated to make a bargain. Towards sundown, I walked off a little distance from the store, thinking it was about time for the gentry to pass by. I ought to have mentioned before, that from some inquiries I had made in Boston, from a countryman of mine, who was a servant in a gentleman's family, I found out that there was a carriage, with three gentlemen, going out to the Governor's. I intended to attack that, if I could fall in with it; —supposing that, at night, they would not be anxious to give fight, after having drank a few glasses of wine—besides, it was probable that I could make a better haul than upon a single person.

When I left the shop, I walked leisurely about, in the direction of the Governor's house, which I was informed of at the tavern. I stood along side the fence some time, keeping a bright look out. I saw many people pass each way, but they were not the quality that I was after. At last, I saw a genteel horse and chaise, with a lady and gentleman in it. I thought something handsome might be lifted there. As soon as the chaise had passed me, I came back to the shop where I had left my horse, mounted him, and set off at full speed, after the chaise. When the coast was clear, and I observed but few people on the road, I overtook the chaise, and commanded the gentleman, (who I have since found to be Major Bray,) to stop; I presented the pistol, and demanded his money or his life.

I do most solemnly declare, that the pistol I presented to Major Bray, *was not loaded.* It had been loaded for some weeks; and that morning, on the road from Salem, I wanted to prove it, and discharged it at a cat on the turnpike. The pistol *was not cocked*, when I shewed it to Major B.

The lady began to conceal her watch-chain. I

MEDFORD, MASS: THE ROAD FROM THE SOUTH

told her not to be uneasy—that I never robbed ladies. He took out his pocket book, and handed me a small roll of bills, amounting to *twelve* dollars, and declared, upon his honor, it was all the money he had. He begged of me that I would be so honorable and generous, as to let him have the notes and papers. I said they were of no use to me, and he might keep them. After he had put up his pocket book, I demanded his watch—which he delivered instantly. The other circumstances attending this robbery, were as related by Major B.

on the trial; "only he forgot to mention, that he was very much frightened, and trembled like a leaf." I shook hands with him, and bid him good bye.

After leaving him, I got off as fast as possible, taking an opposite direction from Medford. I went into a field some distance from the road, where I remained out of the way of observation, for nearly an hour. Here I loaded the pistol that I had presented to Bray. I then came into the main road, and met a handsome chaise, with a large grey horse. It was nearly dark, and I could not distinguish who was in it until I got close to it. I then perceived that it was a negro man and woman. I told him, in a loud voice, to stop. I then asked, "where is your master?" He replied, "what the devil do you want?" I said, "I will let you know, you black rascal." I had the pistol and reins in my left hand, and was about seizing him with the other—He cried out, and begged me to spare his life. I told him I should not hurt him, and bid him go off.

I then went back to Medford—I went to the tavern; there was a great alarm about the robbery of Major Bray, and as they seemed suspicious of me, I rode off slowly till I got out of their sight, then whipped up. At the end of the village, I saw a number of people collected—it was then so dark that they could not discern my face, and I pulled my hat over my eyes. One of them cried out,

"who goes there?" I made no answer. Two or
three asked again, still following me. They then
set up a shout of "stop thief!" and I pushed off as
fast as the horse would go. I had not proceeded
far, before one of the stirrup leathers broke, and
I fell from the horse. In the fall, I dislocated my
left shoulder. They were close upon me; but I
managed to out run them: I sheered into a field,
back of a brick yard, got into the marshes, and
came towards Cambridge. I got into a small clus-
ter of woods, and did not see that any one was in
pursuit. I then dropped down from fatigue and
the pain in my shoulder. After resting a few moments, I took off my suspenders and cravat, tied
them together, fastened one end to a tree, and the
other to my wrist, and so pulled the shoulder back
to its place: Still it was very painful—I rubbed it
with my stocking. I was, however, able to run a
little, and kept on all that night, avoiding the public roads. I stopped occasionally, to inquire the
road to Albany, or to Worcester. At an apothecary's shop, the next morning, I bought some medicine for my shoulder, and it was well in a few
days. I did not take much rest or refreshment, till
I had got within about six miles of Holliston. I
went into a tavern, called for a dinner, and got
some brandy. While I was drinking, I saw an advertisement sticking up, offering a reward for me:
It was a good description of my person; and I
thought it best to keep out of the way. I walked

slowly out of the house, and as no one seemed to observe me very closely, I went round the house, crossed into the fields, and pushed off with all my might, without the dinner. In the afternoon, I came to Holliston; but was afraid to shew myself. It rained very hard, and I kept in the fields and woods, until dark. In the evening, I went into a school house, through the window, and there got a shelter from the weather. In my way there, I stopped at a small farm-house—I said I was a poor traveller from Canada; they gave me some milk and cold meat and bread. I did not wait to eat; but carried it with me to the school house. I slept here some time; and towards morning I awoke, very much refreshed.

I began to be tired of going on foot, and I thought it was best to lift a horse, if I could find a good one. As soon as it was light enough to see, I went off in search of a horse. There were a number in the different fields; but the great difficulty was to procure a saddle and bridle. I went into a number of barns, and into their houses, but could find none. The second house I went to, I got into a kitchen window, and in attempting to go out by the door, I went into a room where a man and woman were asleep. The man awoke, and asked who was there, I answered, "it is me, sir," in a low tone, and he said no more.

I went up to a good looking house, (Mr. Adams',) and after examining in his barn, for a

saddle and bridle, I got into a back window, and
saw a saddle and bridle hanging up in the kitchen.
I took them off without any interruption or noise,
and went in pursuit of a horse, in his field. A large
dog had followed me from another house, and
thinking that I was a suspicious fellow, he kept
up a continual barking. He made so much noise
that I was afraid I should be discovered; and after
I got into the field, I threw a stone at him, and
killed him on the spot. I had brought some corn
in my pocket from one of the barns, and put in my
hat, for the purpose of calling the horse. After
running about some time for him, he came up,
and I put on the saddle and bridle. It proved to
be a fine mare, and carried me very fast to Springfield. I arrived there late in the evening, ordered
my horse to be put up, and after supper I went to
bed, expecting to get up the next morning and
push on to Canada, without molestation. At night
I was awoke by the landlord, who came in with a
sheriff, and a number of other persons, and surrounded the bed. I was so much fatigued from
hard riding, without any refreshment, and not
having rested for some nights, that I slept sounder
than I was aware of. There were so many, and the
alarm was so sudden, that I had no chance for resistance—But if they had given me fair warning,
I should never have been taken alive. The horse
had been traced to Springfield, and at that time the
pursuers knew nothing of the robbery of Major

Bray. I was put in jail that night, and rigidly watched the whole time, until I was committed to the jail at Lechmere Point, Cambridge, for the robbery of Major Bray. The circumstances related on my trial, by all the other witnesses, were strictly correct; and as that is already printed, there is no necessity for repeating them here.

Here Martin's account of himself ends. It was not considered necessary to take his detailed relation, as to any of the subsequent parts of his life, for he had expressed a wish, on Friday, the 7th of December, that the rest might be narrated by his biographer, in as favorable a point of view as was consistent with truth.

On the 9th day of October, 1821, the Supreme Judicial Court sat at Cambridge. On the same day the Grand Jury found a Bill of Indictment against Michael Martin, otherwise called Joseph Hendley, for Highway Robbery, in the first degree. On Friday, the 12th, he was tried and convicted. His deportment throughout his trial, was firm and decent. Some weeks before his trial, Samuel L. Knapp, Esq. of Boston, was requested by Martin's friends, to act as his counsel. He performed this duty with the greatest ability; and although the testimony was uncommonly clear and precise, yet he had the ingenuity and eloquence to create some very strong doubts in the minds of the jury, as to the propriety of convicting Martin cap-

THE CONDEMNED PRISONER IN HIS CELL

itally. Martin always expressed his warmest gratitude for the kindness and exertions of Mr. K. He said, that "he always expected to be convicted of that charge, until he heard the argument of Mr. K.; and then he almost thought himself innocent of the crime." Mr. Parker, of Charlestown, also labored with uncommon industry, in his behalf —but all efforts of his counsel, however zealous, were unavailing. The evidence was so conclusive, that no jury could well avoid such a verdict as was rendered in this case. From the loose manner in which the statute under which he was convicted is expressed, many doubts in the construction of it, might easily be raised. This, too, being the first trial under that statute, and the great point of defence being connected with the uncertain doctrine of mental intent, it was supposed that there might be some misgivings of compassion on the part of the jury. But the testimony was so entire and unimpeachable, and the law being laid down so distinctly by the Court, that there was no possibility for his escape from the verdict of guilty.

In the few days of delay necessarily caused by the motion on his behalf, he had strong hopes that the opinion of the Court might be favorable to him; or at any rate, that he should only be sentenced as of highway robbery in the second degree. More recently, however, he has expressed himself rejoiced, that he was not sentenced to the State Prison for life; and has often declared, that he had rather die the next hour than to meet with such a punishment as perpetual incarceration in the State Prison. When the Chief Justice had pronounced the decision of the Court, upon the questions of law raised by Martin's counsel, and he was asked the usual questions, if he had any thing to say why sentence of death should not then be pronounced against him, he was calm, and answered nothing. The Chief Justice then pronounced the awful sentence, prefacing it with the eloquent remarks which are published in the trial. He stood unmoved, and when the sentence was pronounced, with the most perfect *non-chalance*, took up his hat, saying, "well, that is the worst you can do for me."

During his confinement, he had told all the officers about him, that he should escape if he could, and that he considered himself justified in using every means to save his life. In consequence of his repeated threats, together with some other suspicious circumstances, he was put in irons, about four weeks after his condemnation. The sheriff considered the dungeon in which he was confined, so strong, and confided so much to the vigilance of his keepers, that he considered his escape from it, as utterly impracticable. His good heart revolted at the idea of loading a fellow-being with fetters, unless it was absolutely necessary. Martin was always gay and cheerful; and although visited by many religious and pious people, and by the ministers of the Roman Catholic Church, he never discovered any symptoms of radical penitence, until he had found that he could not easily avoid his fate. He has often said that he did not care how many ministers or other persons came to see him, for it would tend to throw the keepers off their guard, and assist him better to effect his escape.

On the morning of Saturday, the 8th of December, he made a most desperate attempt for his liberty. On Friday, at 2 o'clock, the writer of these pages left him in his dungeon. He was unusually earnest that I should return in the afternoon; but other business prevented. He was confined alone, in a lower room of the stone jail, at Lechmere Point. The dungeon is about eight feet by ten, having no wood work about it; with a thick iron door, fastened by two large bolts, the handles of which, meet in the centre of the door, where they are secured to each other by a large padlock, of very peculiar construction. There was no light or air admitted to this cell, but through three apertures in the wall, each about four inches wide, and twenty long. The entrance was just about wide enough for a common sized man to enter, and is within six feet of the massive outer door, which is of iron also. He was confined to a ring bolt in the centre of the cell, by a large chain, appended to the left foot—the clasp on the ancle, to which it was attached, being very large and heavy.

This chain was also connected with another, attached to his right hand, the links of both being about half an inch in diameter. The chain was sufficiently long to permit him to move all round the room, excepting to go near the door and windows. He had a small stove, which kept him as comfortable as the dampness of the vault would permit, which, together with a straw bed, were placed within his reach. He was very kindly attended, and his appetite was always gratified through the humanity of the jailer, Mr. Train, and his assistant, Mr. Cooledge. He was forbidden nothing but ardent spirits, but had as much wine as was considered necessary for him.

On Saturday morning, December 8, the turnkey, Mr. Cooledge, came in at the usual hour, to make his fire; he was attended by one or two others. Martin was then covered with a great coat, was sitting in his chair, and apparently vomiting. He complained of having been very unwell during the night, and spoke in a very languid tone. He requested of Mr. C. to bring him some wine. The latter went out, still fastening the door after him, and returned in a few minutes, with the wine, attended as before. In about twenty minutes after this, Cooledge came the third time, with his breakfast. He was then unaccompanied by any other person. Martin was then standing up, with the great coat over his shoulders, trembling very much, and rattling his chains. Cooledge sat down his breakfast on a small table near him, and was about leaving the cell, when Martin slyly pulled down a paper of tobacco, which was on the table, and then said, in a feeble voice, " Mr. Cooledge, will you please to pick up that paper of tobacco, I am so weak that I can't stoop." The other very kindly stooped for the purpose, and Martin at the same moment raised the chain by which his hand had been confined, and which he had cut off some days before, and struck Cooledge a most violent blow over the head, which brought him to the ground—He remained insensible for some minutes. Martin then threw off his coat, put on his hat, and pushed out of the jail. He ran with great violence against a gate, which was about ten yards from the outer door of the jail. This gate was made of thick double boards, placed transversely, and strongly nailed. It was fastened on the inside, with a large padlock, attached to a very stout clasp and staple. Martin threw the whole force of his body against it four successive times, without success, running some distance back every time. When he came out of the jail, there was a young man in the jail-yard, who immediately gave an alarm in the house.

After the fourth attack upon the gate, he bethought himself that he had made a great mistake, in not fastening Cooledge in the dungeon, and was returning for that purpose; but he heard the outcry from the women and children in the house—"Martin's gone! Martin's gone!"—and he then made his last desperate leap at the gate. It yielded this time, and every thing was forced away, locks, hinges and all. At the same moment, Cooledge had recovered himself, and came to the outer door, just in time to see Martin break down the gate. The alarm had become general; and at that hour in the day, rendered his escape difficult; for it happened that a number of workmen were returning from their breakfast, in the neighborhood of the jail. However, he went through a barn-yard, in the rear of the jail, over a fence into a corn-field, where he was overpowered by numbers, and taken, after knocking down one or two of his pursuers. The first person who grappled with him, was Cooledge, and he kept firm hold of him until he was supported by the rest. Martin had ran about one hundred yards from the jail-yard. He was securely tied, and brought back to another room, until stronger fetters were forged for him. He was here closely guarded and hand-cuffed; and displayed not the slightest degree of sorrow for attempting to get away: but from that time to the day of his death, always expressed his strong regret that he should have at all injured Cooledge; and said to the last hour of his life, that he had prayed the night before, most earnestly, that he might not kill C., but only disable him, so that he might prevent his pursuing him.

As soon as the narrator heard of the attempted

escape, he went over to the jail, and was left alone some time with Martin. He had refused to tell the officers or the sheriff, the manner in which he unshackled himself, or the true means, by which he became possessed of the tools, to effect the purpose. He still insisted, that he should do every thing in his power, to escape; and told them they must watch him very sharply, or he should give them the slip again. He explained to me the manner of his escape. That before he was put in irons, a good friend of his, had thrown him a case knife and a file into the window: That the knife was of most excellent temper; and that he had employed his leisure moments in manufacturing it into a saw. This he kept concealed, sometimes about his person, and sometimes in a crevice between the stones of the floor, which he would cover over with a kind of paste, that passed very well for mortar; and evaded all investigation. With this saw, he cut off the second link from his ancle, taking out a piece about an inch long. It was cut on both sides of the link, transversely; and before it was quite sawed off, it was broken, so that it should be a little jagged and hold into the link, when he chose to rattle his chains. He selected the second link, because he supposed that the first one would be examined with more accuracy than the rest. The key which confined the iron upon his wrist, he had filed off in the first instance, and could take it out, and liberate his right hand, at pleasure. It was so nicely done, and he had managed it so well, that the strictest examination could not discover that it had ever been removed.

The chains were examined frequently, sometimes twice or thrice a day, by the sheriff, the keeper, and a smith, and no fracture could be detected. On Wednesday preceding his escape, his chains were cut off, and he was removed for the sake of security, and to cleanse his dungeon, into an upper room. Yet throughout all this close investigation, there was no suspicion that he could possibly break from those irons. The smith pronounced them perfectly safe, and he was recommitted to his cell at evening, with every belief in his security. He told me that his chains were cut at the time they removed him into the upper room, and that the interstices in the link were filled up with a composition, which he had prepared of tallow and coal dust. This was so ingeniously put in, and was so much of the color of iron, that the strictest scrutiny was not able to detect it. He observed that they did not understand their business, or they would have either changed his irons every week, or else have struck each link with a hammer, when they examined them. At this time, he seemed to think that escape was impossible; he knew they would guard him close, but he hoped he should not be treated cruelly in consequence of the attempt. He said that he had made only one mistake, which was, in not fastening the door of

the cell upon Cooledge, for he was the first man
that came up to him—That it was impossible for
him to attempt to escape at night, because there

THE PRISON IN WHICH MARTIN WAS CONFINED

was a guard, with loaded muskets and bayonets, at
the door of the prison. The reasons he gave for
the failure were, that he had been so long confined that he had not the perfect use of his legs;
that the clasp on the ancle, and the link appended
to it, impeded his progress, and prevented him
from running as fast as he used to do; besides
which, he had to carry the chain on his hand,
which weighed about 17 pounds. He was induced
to take this with him for purposes of defence, he
said, although he might have easily disincumbered
himself of it.

He was put back at evening, into his old cell,
and bound down to the floor, with a much larger
and stronger chain, besides being hand-cuffed.

He said frequently to the keepers, that notwithstanding they considered themselves sure of him, yet if they would give him a month longer, he would have another chase with them.

From this time, he was most closely guarded— The door of his cell was never opened without a number of attendants, and the utmost caution was observed in the admission of visitors to him. There was a sensible alteration in his manner and feelings, when he found that escape was impossible. He had formerly wished for the company of the religious, and the clergymen of other denominations, who had, no doubt, from the best of motives, and with christian feeling, solicited to visit him; but he now zealously expressed his wish to be visited only by those ministers of the church of which he was born a member. He said one day, very seriously, when I was alone with him, that he "really was sorry that he had not been a good Catholic, and followed the religious and moral instructions that he had received in his youth; that he had neglected the ordinances and faith of his church; and reposed a full and implicit confidence in the directions and advice of Bishop Cheverus."

At this time, he spoke with great calmness, and apparent sincerity, of the advice which he had received from the Bishop; and said, with tears in his eyes, that if he "had been blessed with the directions of such a man, when he was young, he should never have ended his days on a gallows."

He had very serious moments, when he was left to himself, or was alone with his confidential friends: But he often regretted, that when people who were strangers to him, or those who were permitted to approach him, out of mere idle curiosity, would draw him into conversation, that then his thoughts would be diverted from serious subjects. From the third day after his attempted flight, to his execution, he had been trying, when he was left alone, to make up his mind to die: He believed it was the best relief for him; and that an escape, or a commutation of punishment, would only subject him to greater troubles. Whenever any thing was said to him by strangers, about a reprieve, he would oppose it. He said that his crime would be punishable with death in his own country, and that he was ready to meet it here: "the sooner the better."

During the last ten days of his life, he exhibited a wonderful degree of resignation and fortitude; so much so, as to appear romantic and unreal. He would converse with any one, most unreservedly, who came to the prison; and it is to be regretted that there were so many who were permitted to approach him; for these frequent visits tended to abstract his thoughts from more serious subjects. He evinced the greatest calmness in conversing about his last hour, and often about his acceptance with God. But having it so often enjoined upon him, that it was only by a sincere re-

pentance, that his sins could be pardoned—that
he should die in peace and charity with all mankind, and rely upon the promises and atonement
of a Saviour—he then began to have a religious
confidence;—which was, to the last moment, apparently, most sincere. There was no whining or
cant when he talked seriously of death; and his
conduct in his last days, was equally removed from
levity and bravado.

He seemed to be much affected at the distress
which the news of his untimely end would give
to his family in Ireland: and frequently expressed
himself happy that his parents had not lived to
witness his disgrace. He was questioned most
strictly, by several respectable gentlemen of Boston, at different times, whether the detail of his
life, which he had given to me, was correct. He
as often avowed, in the most solemn manner, that
he had given to me nothing but truth, so far as his
memory served him. He said once, that "there
was no need of telling a lie, at this time; it will
only help to keep me back from Heaven." In-
deed, he once said to a friend of his, that if there
was any error, it was that he had not made his life
so bad as it really had been. This same friend, on
the Sunday previous to his execution, went into
his cell—He had not seen him since condemnation—He said to him, "Michael, how does this
world seem to you now?" "Oh!" said he, "like

a column of smoke over the city, which the first gust of wind will drive away."

During the week of his execution, he was very quiet and serious, excepting when his attention was called off by the curiosity and conversation of those who were permitted to enter the jail-yard. He received the unremitting attention and kindness of the Rev. Mr. M'Quade, of the Roman Catholic Church, from the time of his imprisonment, to the moment of his death, with the exception of a few weeks, when the reverend gentleman was obliged to undertake a journey to Canada. His affection for him, was often feelingly expressed, and he endeavored to profit by his religious advice and friendly attention. He had also been most kindly attended by the Rev. Mr. Taylor, of the same church, and more particularly was he thankful for the assiduous and paternal care of the Bishop. On the Wednesday before his death, the Bishop administered to him the holy rite of confirmation, together with the last sacrament. From that moment, he was as tranquil and resigned in his mind, as his body is now quiet in the grave.

On the morning of his execution, he exhibited the same coolness and religious submission that had marked his conduct for some days before. He conversed much about the sins of his past life, and the justice of his ignominious punishment: That if his life should be extended for a few more years, it would only be to add new crimes to those which he had already committed; and that he was now willing to die. He said, that there was no person living, against whom he felt any animosity; and that he died in peace with all mankind. He made all his prayers in the most composed manner; and said that he now placed his confidence only in his God. He continued walking about the room, after his irons were taken off, for the purpose, as he said, of getting the use of his legs. "I should not like to appear awkward; and I would wish that the multitude might see, that I am not afraid to appear before my God. I wish they could see my heart, and know how well I have repented of my sins."

His great anxiety seemed then to be, and he always expressed it with great earnestness, that his body should not be given over for dissection. He was often promised, that every legal step should be taken, to enforce his dying request; and having been reassured of it, on the fatal morning, he seemed very much gratified, and said, "well; I shall die easier for that." He frequently looked through the aperture of the dungeon, to see the concourse of people coming over the bridge: Some of them appeared to be women; and he expressed himself astonished and sorry, that any female should ever be present as such an awful spectacle. He felt very grateful for the attention of the sheriff, and of the keepers. He was particularly mindful of Mr. Cooledge; and rejoiced that he had not done him a more serious injury, when he made the attempt to escape. General Austin had informed those about him, that he should take the prisoner to the place of execution, at fifteen minutes before twelve. A few minutes before that hour, he calmly said, "it is about time that I should make a prayer to my God." There was no person in the cell with him, but his father-confessor, and the writer of this life. After the usual prayers of the church were made, and in which he joined with great devotion, he arose from his knees with cheerfulness, and apparent resignation. In fact, during the whole morning he had never made one discontented or unchristian expression: All was submission, good nature, fortitude, and penitence. Before the hour arrived, he asked for a looking glass, and examined his face two or three times, and adjusted his clothes, and hair, as well as his pinions would permit, with perfect composure. I then asked him if the relation of his life, which he had made to me, was correct and true. He answered, most solemnly, that it was. He was led out, about twelve o'clock, and met his fate with most perfect composure and fortitude; not unmixed with a consciousness that he had met a just doom; and with a humble reliance on the mercy of God, for remission and forgiveness.

The following account, from the Columbian Centinel of Saturday, the 22d December, is here subjoined, as being the most exact which I have seen, and which is corroborated by the sheriff, and all those who were on the scaffold at the time. It was said in a daily paper of Friday, that Martin died with "trepidation" and "emotion"—The following statement is most correct, and the falsity of the other can be testified to by "a cloud of witnesses."

"On Thursday last, MICHAEL MARTIN, was executed for highway robbery, a short distance from the jail, of Middlesex County, in Cambridge, (Lechmere Point,) directly in view from the westerly part of this town, and the State Prison in Charlestown.

"Some time before the execution, he was released from his irons, and was visited in his room by the Rev. Mr. M'Quade, of the Catholic Church. About 12 o'clock, he was put into a close carriage, in which were Sheriff Austin, the reverend gentleman, above named, and a professional gentleman of this town. The carriage was preceded, and surrounded by Deputy Sheriffs on horseback, and followed by a cart containing the criminal's coffin. When arrived at the gallows, the prisoner ascended to the stage, on which the platform of execution was erected, without assistance; and with the most placid look, cast his

The Execution at Letchmere Point, Cambridge

eyes over the immense multitude which surrounded him. He appeared a young man, about 27, in
perfect health, dressed in a suit of black, with a
white neck-cloth, and apparently, the most un-
affected person on the stage, of which there were
nine—the sheriff, the prisoner, the priest, the professional gentleman alluded to, two surgeons, and
three deputy sheriffs. His resignation appeared
unforced. While the sheriff was reading the death
warrant, the prisoner was in earnest conversation
with the priest, and did not appear to hear it. The
warrant having been read, the sheriff announced
to the assembled spectators, that the last office of
religion would be performed to the unhappy man,
by the clergyman then present, and beseeched
them to attend with the same silence and decorum
which they had attended to the reading of the
warrant. The request was fully complied with;
and the utmost silence was preserved while the
priest and the convict, kneeling at the foot of the
steps which led to the scaffold, recited the prayers
of the church, suited to the occasion; Martin re-
sponding with serenity, and frequently making
the sign of the cross. This service ended, the prisoner, the sheriff, and Mr. Train, the gaoler, ascended the scaffold. Martin surveyed the appara-
tus for his execution, for a moment, without any
change of countenance, and then untied his neck-
cloth, and appeared to assist in fixing the fatal
noose to his neck, so as to occasion his death with-

out suffering. He then took a handkerchief, and after the cap was placed over his face, and the sheriff and his deputy had descended to the stage, inquired, with a firm voice, "*When shall I drop the handkerchief?*" The sheriff answered, "*When you please.*" Martin slowly raised his hands thrice to his breast, as in prayer, and then threw down the handkerchief, and was instantly launched into eternity. His death appeared to be immediate, and without suffering. After hanging the usual time, his body was disposed of, as desired in his will. This was the first execution, under the law making the crime, of which Martin was convicted, capital; and the regularity and decorum with which it was conducted, must have made a deep impression on the great body of spectators which witnessed it, and inspired them with a suitable awe of the energy and majesty of the law."

MARTIN was a remarkably well proportioned man, about five feet, nine inches in height; he had a very expressive face; his complexion fair, and his features indicating rather good nature than malignity. An uncommonly piercing blue eye, gave a marked character of intelligence to the possessor, and seemed to crave the pity of the world, that the mind which was there reflected, had not been directed to better purposes. His frame was perfectly formed, and his bones and sinews put together in mighty power. The surgeons who viewed his body, before and after his death, have declared that they had never seen so well made a man. On the day that he committed the crime for which he suffered, he weighed one hundred and eighty four pounds; but he was so symmetrically formed, that the most acute observer would have estimated him at fifty pounds less.

His last will and testament was made the day previous to his execution, and by his direction. The witnesses are well known. As it regards the disposal of his body, his dying request has been rigidly complied with; and it is believed that his corpse has been far removed from the power of surgeons.

If this humble exposition of the life of JOHN MARTIN, will do any good to society, in the way of caution or warning; and if his immortal part may be redeemed and saved by the expiation which he has made for his crimes, by his contrition and penitence, the Compiler of these memoirs will be amply rewarded.

Let no one think that the details of the Life of Martin, have in them any allurements to vice. It is true that such men must always tell their tales in their own way; and crimes are often palliated, disguised, or excused, in their narrations; for it is impossible that a few days of solitary confinement can change their habits of thinking, or give them new feelings, or new motives to action. Their language always remains the same; the cant and mystical terms which ingenious villainy devises, are not easily forgotten; and, in truth, cannot be given up; they are even mingled with the language of contrition and devotion. In the most solemn hour of reflection which passes over the wretched and condemned, who have pursued a course of crime, they seem to one unacquainted with them and their history, to glory in the recollection of past adventures, and to forget their wretchedness in the recital of deeds, however bad, if they have something of bravery in them. It is natural that they should dwell with delight on wonderful escapes from justice. These events are recorded in their memories with the same accuracy, that sieges and battles are in the memories of soldiers, and are often repeated to diminish their apprehensions for the future. But enter the cell of the being, sentenced to expiate his offences against society, on a gallows, and every impression of their satisfaction in the course they have pursued, vanishes—View the felon chained to the floor of his dungeon, shivering with cold, writhing about to make his manacles easier, talking of death, sometimes with horror, at other times with a dogged indifference; then bracing himself up to die bravely, or sinking under the painful thoughts of his own ignominy, and the misery he has brought on others; and then ask yourself, if there is any thing seductive in such a course of life, or any thing attractive in such a scene. Even the prosperous days of a life devoted to crime, are dark and miserable. In the midst of revelry and riot, his mind is in constant agitation and dread— He fears detection, and changes from place to place, from one disguise to another, as often as possible; for he distrusts even his own companions in guilt. His ill-acquired booty is spent without system or prudence, and he plunges forward in desperation, to get rid of his present wretchedness. The way of the transgressor is surely hard, look at it as you will. He lives in the world without sharing any of its solid comforts. He knows that he is out of the pale of society, and that there can be no sympathy with him among the honest part of mankind—All he hopes, is sometimes to excite their admiration by his feats of daring, or to soften their imprecations by a generous deed. A disgrace to every being to whom he claims a kindred tie— Often the cause of the premature death of his parents, the scorn of other relations, he wanders a restless vagabond and an outcast, marked, hunted, and hated, loathing himself.

Can the narrative of such an existence, have a single charm to lead any one, however frivolous or unthinking, to a course of crime? Who would aspire to be the associate of a wretch, driven from place to place, to shun the thief-taker; flying from one country to another, to escape detection — watching every newspaper and hand bill, apprehensive that it contains a reward for his head. There is nothing for him to enjoy—there is every thing for him to suffer—For when his course of crime is finished, and he is ready to suffer an ignominious death—when resentment comes mingled with pity, and the humane attempt to take off the poignancy of his distress, and the pious to prepare him for a better world, by leading him to penitence and prayer, his calmness is generally stupefaction, or desperate courage arising from pride, and his religious hopes spring principally from the novelty, to him, of contemplating religious subjects—He dies unpitied and unwept; and is only remembered as a warning to others, to shun the paths of profligacy and vice.

MARTIN'S WILL IS HERE SUBJOINED

In the name of the Father, of the Son, and the Holy Ghost—Amen.

I, John Martin, commonly called Michael Martin, a native of Ireland, and at present, an inhabitant of the jail at Lechmere Point, in the County of Middlesex, and Commonwealth of Massachusetts, being now under sentence of death, and of sound disposing mind and memory; and expecting in a short time to exchange this world, as I humbly hope, for one that is happier and better; do hereby ordain and publish this instrument, to be my last Will and Testament.

I trust that the Almighty God, against whose precepts and commands I have so often wilfully offended, will remember my sins in mercy: that he will enable me to repent of the many transgressions I have committed, both against his laws and the institutions of civil society; that through the influence and mediation of his consubstantial Son Jesus Christ, who died for the unjust as well as for the righteous, I may be brought to a sincere repentance of my sins, before I go hence; and that my soul may be redeemed and saved by him, who suffered for me.

I do hereby express my regret for the utter disregard I have ever shewn for the doctrines and precepts of that church of which I was born a member, and in which faith my ancestors lived and died—I now declare my belief in the Holy Roman Catholic Church, trusting that, through God's grace, I may die a penitent member of it.

I request of my spiritual directors, the Right Reverend JOHN CHEVERUS, Bishop of Boston, and the Reverend PAUL M'QUADE, a Priest of the Church of the Holy Cross, in Boston, that they would take the charge and direction of all my worldly affairs; and would see that all manner of property, which I now hold, or which is any where within my knowledge or control, may be restored to the lawful owners, if they can any where be found. A true schedule of this property, I have already furnished them; and I hope that those people who have been unjustly treated by me, will have their property restored, as soon as circumstances will permit.

Having thus disposed of all my worldly goods, and feeling much repugnance that my body should be given over for dissection, or fall into the hands of the surgeons—therefore,

I do hereby bequeath my body to FRANCIS W. WALDO, of Boston, Esquire, trusting to his friendship for me, that he will see it decently interred, and preserve it, as far as possible, from molestation.

I take this opportunity to express my sincere thanks to General AUSTIN, the Sheriff of the

County of Middlesex, for his great kindness and attention to me during my imprisonment; as also my gratitude to SAMUEL L. KNAPP, Esq. my counsel, for his able exertions in my behalf, and L. M. PARKER, Esq. who so generously assisted him.

Dated at Cambridge, in the County of Middlesex, this nineteenth day of December, in the year of our Lord one thousand eight hundred and twenty one.

(SIGNED)   JOHN MARTIN.

This instrument was executed in our presence, and declared by the said Martin, to be his last Will and Testament—ISAAC TRAIN, SULLIVAN BALL, NATHANIEL COOLEDGE.

NOTICE.

In order to correct any erroneous impressions as to the property left by Martin, it is proper to state that no money or effects of any kind, have ever been in the possession of the executors named in the preceding will. To prevent any unnecessary inquiries, it is also proper to inform the public, that the only property over which Martin had any control, is the following, viz.:

The Horse taken from Stacy Hall, of Portsmouth, is in the possession of John Clifford, who lives at Latorch, within five miles of La Prairie, Canada.

The Chaise taken from a meeting house, between Londonderry and Newburyport, was left in the neighborhood of Crowninshield's factory, at Danvers. A description of this chaise, is left at the Boston Gazette Office: whoever has lost a chaise, may apply there for the description of it.

A chestnut colored Horse, taken between Montreal and Kingston, about 18 miles from the latter, from an old English gentleman, was left at Burlington, Vermont.

This is all the property of Martin's that his executors know any thing about.